HOW TO
STEAL THE
MONA LISA

HOW TO
STEAL THE
MONA LISA

AND SIX OTHER WORLD-FAMOUS TREASURES

TAYLOR BAYOUTH

A PERIGEE BOOK

PERIGEE
An imprint of Penguin Random House LLC
375 Hudson Street, New York, New York 10014

Illustrations by Denise Au, except pages 49, 69, and 91 by Ross Felten

Library of Congress Cataloging-in-Publication Data
Bayouth, Taylor.
How to steal the Mona Lisa : and six other world-famous treasures / Taylor Bayouth.
pages cm
ISBN 978-0-399-17507-7 (paperback)
1. Art thefts. 2. Theft from museums. 3. Art thefts—Humor. I. Title.
N8795.B37 2016
364.16'287—dc23   2015034989

First edition: March 2016

PRINTED IN THE UNITED STATES OF AMERICA

1   3   5   7   9   10   8   6   4   2

Text design by Spring Hoteling

Most Perigee books are available at special quantity discounts for bulk purchases for sales promotions, premiums, fund-raising, or educational use. Special books, or book excerpts, can also be created to fit specific needs. For details, write: SpecialMarkets@penguinrandomhouse.com.

For my daughters, Zoe and Eliana,
and my loving wife, Beth.

Disclaimer: The material within is intended to be a parody. Please do not attempt any of the techniques or heists detailed herein.

CONTENTS

CONTENTS

PART III: The Aftermath | 189

IT STARTS WITH THE PURCHASE OF THIS BOOK

To successfully carry out the campaigns in this book you will need to practice discretion at every turn—and that starts with the purchase you just made. If someone noticed this book in your possession and was able to draw a connection between you and a crime at some later date, you could inadvertently lead the Feds directly to your own door. Reading through these pages in public, talking openly about the ideas within, or even leaving the book in plain view could be the misstep in an otherwise successful multimillion-dollar payout. Therefore, I urge you to take cautionary steps from the very beginning—and that starts *now*.

Here are some questions to consider before getting started:

- Are you reading this where people or cameras can see you?
- Was the book purchased using cash? Or a traceable credit card?

- Have you been doing research on an encrypted Internet connection?
- Is there anyone close to you with insight into your personal interests and who might attempt to sabotage you if the opportunity arose?

Be aware that it is often details like these that are overlooked early on that land even the brightest criminal masterminds behind bars. The practice of discretion must begin *now* as cautiousness is the most critical element in keeping the perceived distance between you and the crime at an absolute maximum.

PRUDENCE OVER VIOLENCE

Let's be clear: None of the campaigns in this book requires violence of any kind, whatsoever. A seasoned thief should never have to slip a dioxin tablet into a security guard's coffee or threaten a witness to keep his or her mouth shut or torture a security administrator for a username and password. If you follow each step laid out for you in this beat-by-beat companion guide, you should be able to get away with stealing some of the world's most valuable and iconic treasures without having to inflict harm on anyone.

As long as you maintain a professional approach, always paying close attention to the details, you have every chance at success. If not, expect to bear the consequences: Life imprisonment, or worse.

In Part I, we'll start by going over the basics. I cover topics like disguise, breaking and entering, how to employ a team, and the meticulous art of casing your targets. Let's get started.

PART I
THE BASICS
OF THIEVERY

Becoming Invisible

THE ART OF DISGUISE

These days there are cameras everywhere: on street corners, in shops and buildings, and on people's cell phones. In fact, it's nearly impossible to find a place where your face *isn't* being recorded. Because you always want to create distance between your true identity and the crime, you'll want to master some techniques to create a disguise that you can slip into at a moment's notice and one that doesn't require excessive gear or preparation.

For men: If possible, begin with short hair and a clean-shaven face. This will be more flexible and will allow you to change your look using wigs, mustaches, beards, and so on; these are all good ways to alter your appearance quickly and with less risk of someone spotting a poorly matched hairpiece.

For women: While there is no need to shave your head (as-

suming it isn't shaved already) it's generally wise to start *blond*. Blond hair is much easier to dye darker and is less likely to be noticed under a wig. However, if blond hair does not match your skin tone, better to stay dark. Length is important too. Women's hair should be short enough to hide with a wig or long enough to pull back into a ponytail or tight bun. Anything in-between is going to be difficult to work with.

Wigs are a great way to change your look without a lot of work. Find a good one, not one of those plastic wigs you wear for Halloween. Find a wig shop and get fitted with several high-quality synthetic wigs with *lace fronts*, which will give the illusion of natural hair growth along the hairline. In addition, it's critical that your hair color matches your eyebrows. Use colored brow gel that's quick to apply and washes off easily.

Clothing and accessories are excellent tools that you can use to enhance the look of your character. You want to blend in as much as possible so be sure to remove identifiable logos, designs, patterns, or markings. When the job is done you will lose the wig, cut or dye your hair, toss away spectacles, change your clothes—whatever you can do quickly and easily to change your appearance and be able to leave the scene without being recognized. During the reconnaissance phase, however, you must wear your new disguise at all times. No exceptions.

FAKE IDENTIFICATION

A good disguise on its own is simply not going to cut it. You're going to have to develop the essence of your character in case you get stuck engaging in a conversation with an unsuspecting person mid-heist. Choose a persona that reminds you of someone you already know; this will help you in taking on various characteristics without having to think too much.

For further reading on character development, pick up a copy of *An Actor Prepares* by Constantin Stanislavski. Leveraging the *method* technique can be a valuable tool that can turn a potentially bad situation around.

Once you feel confident in your new character, you can begin the search for a forger. Forgers can be found anywhere but generally lurk in low-income areas where you can find a disproportion of liquor stores, hole-in-the-wall bars, pawnshops, bail bondsmen, and the like. The trick is to frequent areas like these in order to gain the trust of locals and ultimately work up the courage to start asking around. Don't forget, you are in disguise, so even if someone becomes suspicious and reports you to the police they will be describing someone who doesn't even exist.

A fake driver's license will set you back only around $160, depending on where you are and the quality of the work. However, if you're traveling internationally you can expect to pay anywhere between $7,000 and $10,000 for a counterfeit passport. Quality is of the utmost importance here, and so the better you get to know the underbelly of the city you are in and its shady inhabitants, the more likely you are to find a professional that can provide you with the real deal.

FINGERPRINTS AND OTHER IDENTIFYING TRACES

There is no worse feeling than pulling off a crime only to realize you left behind an identifiable trace to lead authorities directly to your doorstep. Something as seemingly insignificant as a thread of your clothing, a strand of your hair, or even a fingerprint, while invisible to the naked eye, can bring an otherwise flawless operation crashing down.

Let's start with fingerprints, as they are often overlooked and generally misunderstood. The only thing a fingerprint proves is that a specific individual was present and touched something; a damning oversight indeed if the suspect had no reason to be wherever the print was left. However, museums and public places are littered with prints like these. Does visiting the Louvre in Paris make you a criminal or simply an innocent art lover? That being said, wearing a pair of latex gloves is never a bad idea, especially when you are working in areas with polished surfaces or to which the public has no access.

Buttons, threads, pieces of fabric, and other microscopic remnants can all be your ultimate undoing if not properly considered. For instance, fiber transfer, a common exploitation by forensics teams, can be easily avoided by wearing common fabrics. The world produces approximately eighty billion pounds of fabric every year, about half of which is cotton. Black cotton is generally preferred among seasoned criminals as it absorbs light, provides full range of motion, and is so common that it is virtually untraceable. In addition, remove ahead of time buttons, straps, zippers, tags, and anything else that might catch on something, or become detached.

Hair, fingernails, blood, and other DNA-rich traces are potentially traceable, but keep in mind that unless your DNA is stored somewhere and linked to a *previous crime*, you might be overthinking it. However, below are some simple steps you can take to avoid shedding anything lab-worthy.

- Shave or cover long hair with a hairnet.
- Facial hair and even excessive body hair should be shaved.
- Keep your fingernails shortly trimmed.

- Take any trash you've accumulated on site that might contain saliva, blood, urine, or excrement with you.
- Wear latex gloves when working in areas with high-gloss surfaces.

USING THE INTERNET, ANONYMOUSLY

Modern-day out-of-the-box browsers are simply not secure, but there are other options for communicating over the Internet anonymously. Tor is an *encrypted* browser that directs Internet traffic through an anonymous global network consisting of more than four thousand relay hosts, which conceal a user's location and transmitted information from anyone conducting network surveillance. Using a browser like Tor will allow you to connect with individuals and groups operating on the black market, without the worry of leaving a trail. No matter if your transmission gets into the wrong hands, it can never be traced back to you. Be sure to use an encrypted browser for all instances of web use mentioned in this handbook.

OUTSMARTING SURVEILLANCE

Countersurveillance refers to any measures undertaken to prevent surveillance. Most bug surveillance devices emit some form of electromagnetic radiation, usually radio waves, that while undetectable by a person can be easily identified using technical surveillance countermeasures (or TSCM) techniques. TSCMs allow you to examine—or *sweep*—a designated area in an attempt to discover electronic eavesdropping devices. To do this you really need only one tool: the CPM-700 Countersurveillance Probe/Monitor. The CPM-700, which sells for around $2,000, will allow you to quickly and quietly ferret out all types of sophisticated eavesdropping devices, including audio and video transmitters, and even old tape-driven systems.

The CPM-700 can pick up electronic noise from up to twenty feet away and comes with a directional *hot mic* that can be used to pinpoint exactly where a camera or other recording device is hiding. You should carry out sweeping and other countersurveillance measures several weeks before your planned campaign. This will allow enough elapsed time so anyone that happens to see you (and potentially finds you suspicious) will have forgotten you. However, you don't want to carry out countersurveillance measures too early and miss a newly installed camera or audio bug. That would be an unfortunate surprise.

Identifying surveillance is really only the first step. Next you will need to know how to *disable* these systems—or at the very least, get around them without being spotted. There are many clever gadgets you can use for obstructing audio and video surveillance, but the cheapest and most practical is a can of Silly String. This technique works well as the aerosol string can easily reach a target up to twenty feet away. The foamy string itself is a sticky opaque substance that can blind a camera quickly with less risk of triggering an alarm. (Versus breaking the device, which could trigger an alarm). This technique will work for audio surveillance as well as it will muffle microphone inputs and distort the recording.

These methods of uncovering and disabling surveillance systems are common practice for any heist you carry out. Always assume you are being watched and/or listened to. Next to being caught in the act, being identified on record is the absolute worst thing that can happen.

Techniques and Tools of the Trade

When thinking about bypassing security, either for a building or a safe, it helps to think of the problem in terms of concentric spheres that must be penetrated in a certain order to gain you access to the center. To bypass these barriers—which might include picking locks, cutting through glass, or scaling walls—you need an armory of tools and techniques at your disposal to help disable or circumvent all potential layers of security.

LOCK PICKING

Like many techniques in this book, lock picking is more art than science. While the steps I give will help you get started in the hobby of lock picking, it is by no means a substitute for *experience*. You want to start by purchasing various types of pin tumbler locks from your local hardware store and practice on those using the tools and the methods in this section. Once you are able to pick a lock in under sixty seconds, you should be ready—any longer than that and you risk being caught.

Keep in mind that this technique will work only with your standard *pin tumbler* lock. Lock picking is by no means a tool for high-security entry. In the "Campaigns" section of this book, we will cover in detail the exploitation of custom, state-of-the-art security systems. For now, however, getting through your typical door lock is a boilerplate skill any thief should have mastered.

First, a little about how these locks work: A pin tumbler lock is composed of a series of spring-loaded stacks called *pin stacks*. Each pin stack is composed of two pins that are stacked on top of each other: the key pin, which touches the key when it is inserted, and the driver pin, which is spring driven. When the different length key pins are aligned at their tops by the insertion of the correspondingly cut key at their bases, the tops of the key pins and, consequently, the bases of the driver pins, form a straight line (the *shear line*), so that the lock can be turned.

Before you get started you will need a tension wrench, a sawtooth rake, and a short hook, which can be found online as part of any traditional lock pick set.

1. Use your tension wrench to depress the lock plug, while simultaneously applying pressure both in a clockwise and counterclockwise movement. You will notice one direction will have more give; this will tell you which direction the lock turns.

2. The sawtooth (or snake rake) is inserted opposite the tension wrench and is designed to lift multiple pins at once. Don't worry

about applying much tension at this point; just push the rake in as far as possible. Once your rake has penetrated the lock you want to apply upward pressure while dragging it out. Do this fairly quickly; there is little finesse necessary when using this tool.

3. Try this method using both clockwise and counterclockwise tension. You are listening for the slight tapping sound of each spring-loaded pin as it pops down. As each pin drops you will notice more and more give from the hand applying pressure to the plug.

KEY BUMPING

Though generally less reliable than lock picking, key bumping works for 90 percent of standard door locks. However, if speed is your focus, there is no faster way to breach your standard door lock than with a bump key. A *bump key* is a blank key that has been specially cut to rake the pins in a lock by simply smacking the back end of the key with a blunt object. This method can force open the pins without the use of a lock pick set, most of the time.

Bump keys can be found online in various shapes and sizes. It is recommended that you have a key ring with a variety of bump keys along with your traditional lock pick set. When confronted with a locked lock, your first tool of choice should be the bump key. It's fast and requires minimum tools. However, without knowledge of traditional lock picking you run the risk of an unbumpable lock and a heist that was over before it began.

GETTING THROUGH GLASS

In the movies cutting through glass is as simple as using a scoring tool and a suction cup to create a perfectly round hole that you can easily fit your arm or body through. However, this isn't the movies, so be warned that scoring stronger glass with your typical diamond-edged glasscutter is nearly impossible.

Unreinforced glass might not take much to get through. You do, however, want to avoid the sound of *breaking* glass, lest you arouse the suspicions of anyone nearby. The sound of a window breaking is not caused by the breaking itself; it's caused by falling pieces of glass hitting each other, and surfaces they fall on. To get around this, keep a few sheets of rolled-up butcher paper and some rubber cement in your backpack. When you find a window free of reinforcement or attached alarms, simply tear off a sheet of paper roughly the size of the window, coat one side with rubber cement, and press it onto the glass. Now simply strike the window with a hammer (or some other blunt object) and voilà—the glass shards will remain stuck to the paper and you've successfully breached the building without making a sound.

For stronger *tempered* glass, a blunt object simply won't be enough. For this you're going to need some power, and power means a bigger, louder job. For these situations you'll use a drill to perforate the glass so it can be easily broken through. When drilling through glass, keep in mind that friction creates heat, and heat can easily melt an iron drill bit. To avoid this you are going to need lubricant to keep the drill bit cool. Water works well for this and should be applied continuously. You can use a water bottle and drill with one hand while lubricating with the other, or you can create a small dam

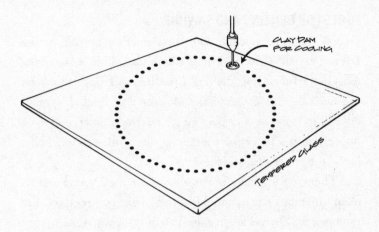

around the drill hole using modeling clay. This method can be effective, especially when both hands are needed to apply force to the drill. Depending on the thickness of the glass, vary the distance between drill holes to weaken the structure so it can be easily penetrated with a mallet or hammer.

For *vertical* glass that you need to drill through you won't be able to use the clay dam technique to keep your drill bit cool. In these situations you'll want to have a water bottle and a small bucket to catch and recycle the water. Just make sure to keep the stream of water on your bit constant.

TOOLS FOR DRILLING AND SAWING

One of the most valuable tools in a thief's repertoire is the Dremel variable-speed cordless rotary tool. This is one of the most powerful cutting, drilling, grinding, and routing tools on the market—and a *must-have* tool for any thief. It's small enough to store on your person; it's relatively quiet; and most important, it's powerful enough to deal with screws, bolts, locks, hinges, plates, and more.

There are so many practical uses for the Dremel and so many situations where a tool like this might be necessary. For example, the Dremel might come in handy for you when:

- Removing panels for entry into a ducting system.
- Boring out stubborn door locks.
- Severing cables to disarm cameras and security systems.
- Sawing off pesky security screws with nonstandard heads.

The drill bits I recommend buying first are the *diamond wheel-cutting blade* and the *cone steel cutter* bit. With these bits you can complete tasks in seconds that would normally take minutes. And in the end, it's *seconds* that will ultimately determine whether you wind up in the riches—or in a federal penitentiary.

THERMITE, FOR THE TOUGH STUFF

Thermite is a composition of aluminum powder, fuel, and metal oxide. When ignited by heat, thermite undergoes an exothermic oxidation–reduction reaction that can generate concentrated molten heat; perfect for burning through hardened-steel encasements that you can access from the *top*, such as a floor hatch or a protruding door lock.

While this method is highly effective for otherwise impenetrable locking apparatuses, use it with extreme caution, as the chemical reaction is strong and potentially very dangerous if proper precautions are not taken.

To make thermite you need to mix 75 percent iron oxide with 25 percent aluminum powder. Use a scale to get your ratios correct or you won't be able to create the heat necessary to destroy the harder, tempered steels. Purchase a small ceramic flowerpot, the kind with a hole in the bottom, and line it with a coffee filter to prevent the thermite from spilling through. Pour the thermite compound into the pot and cover with a thin sheet of tin foil. To use, simply set the pot on any unyielding surface, uncover, ignite, and stand back.

When igniting thermite, the UV radiation can damage your eyes if looked at directly. Make sure you are looking away or wearing welder's goggles to protect your eyes from the potentially blinding light.

Thermite can also be helpful if you need a distraction to aid a tight getaway. In these situations, it's best to ignite using a delayed timer. To do this, use a length of magnesium ribbon, about six inches long. Stick the ribbon into your flowerpot of thermite and light using a butane torch. This setup gives you roughly one minute before things start to heat up.

While there are many ways to break into something, sometimes the smartest thing you can do is climb *over* it. It's time to talk about one of the most iconic and effective tools in a thief's repertoire—the grappling hook.

UTILIZING A GRAPPLING HOOK TO SCALE WALLS AND BUILDINGS

If you've never practiced carrying your own weight on a rope, now would be a good time to try. Take a trip to your local park and see how long you can hang on to the monkey bars with your feet off the ground. If you can't last at least five minutes, you'll want to hit the gym before attempting any of these campaigns.

While there are most certainly other options for getting to high places, the grappling hook takes up less room, weighs hardly anything, and allows you to scale buildings virtually silently.

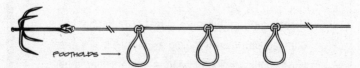

FOOTHOLDS →

To construct a compact grappling hook, complete with rope and footholds, you will need forty feet of climbing rope, two carabineers, a foldable four-fluke steel grappling hook, and three feet of chain. Here's what you need to do.

1. Attach a carabineer to the eye of your grappling hook and clip the opposite end to a three-foot length of chain (the chain will be able to withstand rough edges that might otherwise fray a rope).

2. Attach the second carabineer to the loose end of your chain.

3. Tie one end of your rope to the free end of your chain.

4. Start at the free end of your rope and tie a foothold every two feet from the end of the rope and all the way to the chain so you'll be able to easily reach whatever you're climbing and pull yourself up. The *bowline in a bight knot* (illustrated below) will fasten the footholds, which will help you climb faster and with more control.

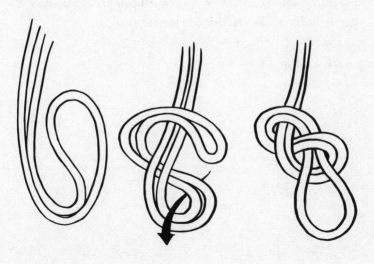

Throwing a grappling hook is relatively straightforward. If you've ever seen a cowboy roping a horse, it's a similar action, only you should be swinging the hook to the side of your body, instead of over your head. Still, it might take a few times to get this right. I'd recommend trying this and getting good at it before incorporating a grapple into any heists. Start by holding on to the loose end of the rope with one hand. Take the other end, where the rope meets the chain, and begin swinging in a circular motion. Shoot for a hard ledge, piping, fire escape—anything that can catch and will hold your weight. Once you have enough momentum to reach the ledge, aim five to ten feet above your target (to compensate for gravity) and release the grapple. Once your grappling hook is attached you can test it by sticking your foot through the first loop and lifting your entire body weight onto the rope. Give it a few solid bounces to make sure that it is properly anchored. The rest is easy. All you have to do now is climb the rope, like a ladder, one loop at a time.

Confidants and Profitable Partnerships

If you don't already know people whom you trust and believe are capable of carrying out a plot to steal a coveted world artifact, there are other channels available to you. It's important to note, that while all of these methods are completely feasible, none of them is foolproof. All of the following techniques rely on your own ability to sniff out those who might attempt to double-cross you. Make the wrong decision, and you could end up losing your fortune, or even worse, staring down the barrel of a gun.

THE MAFIA AND THE UNIONE CORSE

There is no crime safer than organized crime, which is why organizations such as the Italian Mafia and France's Unione Corse are your best bet when looking for trustworthy professionals. These organizations are refined not only in how they circumvent the law (typically by paying them to turn a blind eye) but in how they conduct their business in plain view, accessible to anyone willing to pay the right fee.

Getting close to a senior member of the Italian American Mafia, for instance, is not as difficult as you might think. Take the Gambino crime family who are still active in New York today. While there is currently no prominent godfather within the Gambino family—Francesco Cali turned down the position to remain under the radar—you can still find extended family members who have *direct* connections with the people you're looking for. The work you will put in to traveling, identifying, contacting, and conspiring with members of notorious crime families will be far worth your effort.

When working abroad, you may want to contact local criminal organizations, such as the Unione Corse. The Unione Corse is a secret society and criminal organization operating primarily out of Corsica and Marseilles in France. Historically known as the primary organizers of the French Connection, the monopoly that controlled trade in heroin between France and the United States circa 1970, the Unione Corse is alive, well, and actively looking to make relationships with the right people.

You can seek out members of both groups directly, without worry of leaving a trail, by using an encrypted browser and accessing one of the many Deep Web marketplaces; such as Silk Road, Onion, or Hidden Wiki. These networks allow people to communicate with one another without threat of Internet snooping. However, using a fake identity (at least in the early stages while you are still building relationships) is generally recommended.

If you are skilled enough in the art of trust building, you just might get lucky. This process involves due diligence into the people you are contacting: understanding where they come from, what types of projects they involve themselves with, and demonstrating a deep respect for their cultural and familial ties to the organization they are part of. This kind of social maturity coupled with a carefully laid-out proposal is really all you need to get the right people's attention.

> For high-stakes crimes such as those laid out in the chapters ahead, spending a year (or even more) establishing meaningful bonds should be assumed in order to keep the threat of betrayal at a minimum.

EX-CONVICTS

Ex-convicts are also great resources when planning a complex bust, given that the recidivism rate among criminals is so high. According to the Bureau of Justice Statistics, roughly 68 percent of inmates will be *re*-incarcerated within two months of being released. This means, the odds of finding someone who has been recently released and is willing to jump back into the fray are in your favor.

All of the countries mentioned in this book offer a public, and usually a *permanent,* system to handle queries related to the incarcerated. You can find these national inmate archives by doing a simple web search. Ex-felons are typically cataloged by name, location, race, gender, and a crime index (a unique code assigned to each crime type). This will allow you to narrow your focus to recently released inmates located in the area of your operation with a history of theft. The search should provide enough information to investigate and locate your partners-for-hire. You want to identify at least ten candidates for every team member you need. In other words, you should investigate *ten* people before you hire *one*.

A simple web search on every name on your list will give you a sense of each thief's professionalism and transparency. Filtering is simple: Anyone whom you can learn *nothing* about gets removed; anyone involved in petty crimes, such as grand theft auto or home burglary, gets removed; history of drug abuse? Forget it; previously incarcerated for a violent crime? Don't even bother. You get the idea. Continue to boil the list down by removing the bad until you have the best possible candidates remaining. Those left on your list should be people who have been involved in high-stakes crime such as embezzling funds, heisting jewels, and hijacking rare artwork; these are the people you can employ and, more important, trust.

Once you have a final list you can reach out directly (either by phone, post, and if encrypted, email) and begin to build your relationship. Keep in mind; communication with current or former prisoners is most likely being monitored so you need to be careful. If they're currently incarcerated, your goal is to find out when they expect to be released and if they are interested in meeting with you once they are—nothing else. If you don't have time to wait, move on. If their responses raise too many questions or fail your gut check, they probably aren't the right fit.

PEOPLE YOU CAN EXERT MENTAL CONTROL OVER

Possibly one of the most powerful ways to build up your team is through mentorship and manipulation—that's right, good old fashioned brainwashing. This particular mode of acquiring a trustworthy team takes time, so you must be patient. Having someone you already know well and whom you trust is ideal, although not a prerequisite.

Assuming you have found the right individual and have established his or her conviction, begin testing the waters by casually introducing the idea of a museum hit. "Have you ever thought about doing something really wild, like ripping off a priceless piece of art?" Nonspecific comments like this are a great litmus test for a person's ethical framework and can help demonstrate their allegiance to you. Take note of his or her response and use it to determine whether or not to move forward with the conversation. At the right time you can make the leap by laying out a concrete plan. Don't worry; you can always chalk it up to a joke if the person reacts badly. You want to be sure you don't divulge too much information to someone who may ultimately turn against you, so take your time and learn to look for the right signals.

Since this particular topic is beyond the scope of this book, only the basics are dealt with here. There are many comprehensive books on the subject out there; see *Mind Control Mastery* by Jeffrey Powell for a step-by-step guide on how to manufacture loyalty through manipulation.

Reconnaissance and the Art of the Case

A PLUG-AND-PLAY COMPANION GUIDE (WELL, MOSTLY)

This book gives you an advantage over your run-of-the-mill crime handbooks, as reconnaissance for each mission has already been carried out for you. I've shortened the necessary time frame for each heist by providing detailed analysis of anything worth knowing, including patrol patterns, gaps in security, getaway routes, and territory exploits. With few exceptions, the heists herein are designed to be relatively plug-and-play, meaning the prep work and the laborious process of information collection have already been done and documented for you in a clear and comprehensive manner.

However, this book is by no means a substitute for prudent thinking and thorough planning of your own. The details herein contain factual information related to every aspect of the target and the plan to acquire it. While I have done my best to prepare you sufficiently, it's impossible to predict changes in security, staffing, architectural features, or even the physical location of the target itself (security systems can change, galleries can be renovated, exhibits can be relocated). It is for this reason I recommend conducting your own investigation to identify and address anything new that might affect your plan.

CASING THE JOINT

Perhaps one of the most romanticized criminal undertakings is the alluring reconnoiter; more commonly referred to as, *the case*. Typically performed alone and at night, the case is one of your best tools for covert information gathering. Almost 99 percent of the time allotted to planning each heist should literally be spent *sitting* and *watching*. The process involves detailed surveying and logging of anything relevant, including descriptions and schedules of all key staff members and personnel, makes and models of security and staff vehicles, special service roads and unmarked access points, nearby scheduled construction, local events, upcoming holidays, and anything else that might prove to be valuable to the campaign and your escape.

> In some cases taking a staffed position at the place you are studying is a perfectly reasonable way to garner key information about patterns that occur during working hours and that might not otherwise be available to someone on the outside.

First and foremost you must conduct your work completely unnoticed. The last thing you need is some passerby with a photographic memory rattling off information to the police. You need a generic vehicle, preferably an unmarked van, with tinted rear windows and comfortable seats. Bring with you a pair of 10×50mm antireflective binoculars so you can monitor from afar, protein and water to keep your head sharp, and a GPS device so you can bail quickly without getting lost.

Typically you want to begin by conducting a spot check of the location by driving by a few times to survey the area before permanently setting up shop. Find a place across the street and out of the way of traffic or pedestrians. Once you have found a discreet location, park your vehicle and get into the backseat. There are generally looser laws around tinted *rear* windows, plus people rarely look in the backseat of a vehicle with no driver.

Your job at this point is simple—note *everything* you see. That goes for people in and around the area, what they are wearing, what they look like, visible security systems (such as surveillance cameras), vehicles identified with makes, models, and even license plates if you can manage. Basically you want to capture the patterns and schedules of things and people and you should do so for each day of the week. This is a tedious process that can take weeks to months. It stops only when you can effectively predict what day and time the building you are surveying is most vulnerable. As long as there are surprise visits—cleaning crews, patrol cars, night watch, and so on—your work is not done.

You may be thinking, "What if there are no patterns? What if there are constant surprises?" To that I will say that you simply haven't been patient enough. The world *runs* on schedules. People have jobs with defined shifts, and security systems run on computers, which are all driven by the clock. We eat dinner at the same time. We call the same people. We strive for punctuality (well, most of us). We are creatures of habit, and we run our institutions in the same repetitive manner.

The caveat here is that things *do* change; but when they do you will know. Any unexpected shift leaves you with a decision: Move forward or abandon the campaign altogether? How much risk are you willing to take? This is something only you can decide.

PART II
THE CAMPAIGNS

The Hope Diamond

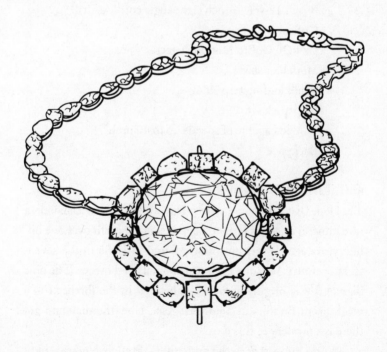

APPROXIMATE VALUE
$250 million

LOCATION
Smithsonian Institution, National History Museum,
Washington, DC, USA

EQUIPMENT REQUIRED
Flush cutters
Grappling hook and rope
Bosch 12-volt ⅜-inch right-angle cordless drill
GoPro camera
CamDo GoPro Motion Detector
Modeling clay
Small folding step stool
Lock pick set
Moped capable of speeds up to 40 mph
Backpack

ABOUT THE HOPE DIAMOND

The Hope Diamond is a large, deep-blue, forty-five-carat diamond—a rare mineral that was formed deep inside the earth over one billion years ago. It was most likely found in India in the seventeenth century, but little is known about its first owner. The blue diamond was originally found embedded in the forehead of a magnificent Buddha in Southeast Asia. How the diamond got there is a mystery to this day.

We do know that in the mid-1600s, French gem merchant

Jean-Baptiste Tavernier joined the monkhood that guarded the diamond in the Ananda Temple. However, Tavernier was not interested in becoming a monk but in getting his hand on the blue diamond. One night, when the head count was particularly low, Tavernier strangled two of the monk guards and grabbed the diamond. Tavernier soon made it out of India, only to be mauled to death and eaten by a streak of tigers.

The history of the diamond doesn't end there. It's changed hands numerous times on its way from India to France to Britain and, finally, to the United States, where it lives today. The diamond has a long history of bringing misfortune and tragedy to its owners and so carries a reputed curse. However, there are strong indications that the diamond's various owners fabricated these stories to enhance the stone's mystery and appeal since, historically, increased publicity has only raised the gem's newsworthiness and value.

OVERVIEW

Stealing the Hope Diamond is a surprisingly straightforward operation, assuming you have the right information and tools. While the National Museum of Natural History is one of the most trafficked and secure museums in the world, it still must operate completely off of federal funding and private donations. This means its vault of treasures is about as secure as your local bank. Keep in mind, while budgets for museums can be in the millions, the sheer square footage means security budgets must be spread very thin. So thin in fact that entering the Smithsonian in the dead of night will be as simple as understanding just a little about its geothermal heating system and the software that controls the museum's security systems.

PROCURING A SAFE HOUSE

Getting in and out of the museum itself is surprisingly the easiest aspect of this particular job. It's navigating the streets of Washington, DC, itself, during what will inevitably be a citywide manhunt, that will undoubtedly be the most challenging part. Due to the extremely high profile of the target, it is to be expected that a ten-mile sweep of the area would go into effect immediately upon authorities being notified of a breach. Given that this particular museum is merely a few city blocks away from the iconic home of the American president, authorities should be expected to act swiftly and with force. It is for these reasons that you will need to secure a nearby safe house in which you can vanish until the heat of America's finest police force cools and allows for a safe and unimpeded escape.

The ideal location lies on the far edge of Washington's Potomac Park, which you can access through Independence Avenue. There, west of the Tidal Basin, you will find many low-rent residencies, homeless persons, and a cluster of inns and motels rarely frequented by police. Such housing not only offers good long-term cover where you can blend in, but it is also easily accessible to the museum.

You will play the role of a down-and-out junkie, a transient to any passersby—just another vagabond looking for a fix and a place to stay warm. Here's what you need to do:

- Your attire should be mangy jeans, a soiled T-shirt, a tattered jacket, and a knit cap.
- Find a low-cost, long-stay motel that accepts cash.
- Avoid prolonged conversation and/or eye contact with anyone.
- Stay indoors and leave only if absolutely necessary.
- Make no calls and no attempts to contact anyone.

For more information on how to develop a believable disguise see "The Art of Disguise" on page 3.

> Before you begin, be sure to have a three-week supply of nonperishable food, drinking water, and whatever else you need for a lengthy stay indoors.

GETTING STARTED

There are three primary weaknesses you will be exploiting to gain entrance to the southeast wing on the second floor of the Smithsonian's National Museum of Natural History:

1. **Dispersed layout:** Security is spread thin due to the sprawling grounds.
2. **Close proximity to escape routes:** The specific location of the Hope Diamond lies roughly a hundred yards from a museum entrance and parallels a

low-traffic intersection by Fourth Street and Pennsylvania Avenue.

3. **Unguarded entryways:** An accessible heating duct that is open throughout winter.

Sometime in early February a groundsman will be instructed to remove a large metal hatch from a four-foot-wide air duct used to transfer heat from an outdoor geothermal heating system positioned on the northwest corner of the museum. Geothermal systems take advantage of the Earth's ability to store vast amounts of heat in the soil. The heat is then transferred to a fan and pushed into large aluminum vents. This system is responsible for heating the Museum of Natural History and the lower floors of the Air and Space Museum. Once the hatch on the main entrance is removed you'll face several low-barrier security measures, which I'll go over in detail in the following section.

PENETRATING THE OUTER PERIMETER

Before going anywhere you're going to need to alter your appearance so your face isn't captured on camera. You don't need to go over the top; it's dark out and this particular surveillance system was installed circa 1980, definitely low fidelity. However, our approach (as usual) is a cautious one, so you will be coming in disguise. A hooded sweatshirt or baseball cap should be sufficient to hide your face. A pair of thick-rimmed glasses wouldn't hurt either as glass tends to reflect and makes it difficult to detect eye color.

You will be arriving on your moped with all of your equipment at around 1 a.m. You are entering on the northwest corner

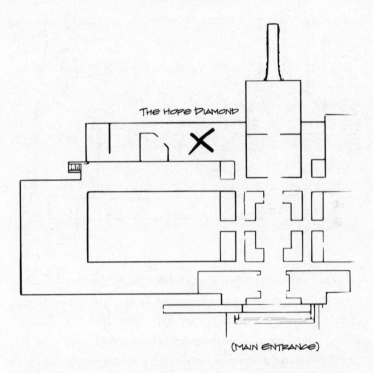

of the Natural History Museum via Constitution Avenue; there will be a visible access road that leads south. Take it, but don't go far. You need to get off of the road and into the trees where there is cover. Park there and hurry quietly toward a large, aluminum structure. This is the industrial heating unit that I mentioned earlier. Take cover behind the west side of the structure. You will see a sign that reads: *Museum Personnel Only.* Be careful! You are officially trespassing at this point. Get caught and you can expect to spend the next six months behind bars.

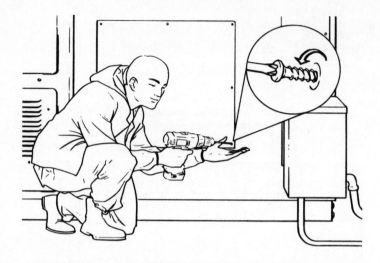

Find the panel marked *Danger: High Voltage Electrical Equipment* and cut off the panel's hinges using your pneumatic flush cutters, then remove the screws with your 12-volt drill (see above). Once you remove the panel, you will find an aluminum grating covering a four-foot duct secured with a simple double-ball locking padlock. Remove the lock with your flush cutters and you are in.

NAVIGATING THE DUCTS

It should take no longer than ten minutes to navigate through the northeast wing and up into the southeast wing on the second floor of the Natural History Museum, where the Hope Diamond is kept. Move quickly and quietly while taking stock of any worrisome sounds coming from inside the building, such as security guards milling about.

You will know when you are there because the main duct will come to a dead end. Notice the narrowed extension at a slight grade ahead of you: There should be more than enough room to fit through, lying stomach down and head first. Start crawling.

There won't be many turns to worry about here as the duct you are in only supplies heat to the northeast and northwest wings on the first and second floors. Once you are in, however, you want to make your first *left* to go in the direction of the Gems and Minerals Hall. Once there you will have only one way to go—up. You should be able to reach the ledge above using your folding stepladder if you are over five feet tall. Give yourself a boost to get your forearms planted in the duct above. Now you can pull yourself up and into the final horizontal stretch of your journey. Your stop is going to be the second access panel on your left—which will take you directly into the geology exhibit and just around the corner from where the Hope Diamond is kept.

Remove the panel with your cordless drill. There should be twelve screws that, once removed, will allow you to easily slide the grating off, giving you direct access into the museum. Be careful though, as you will be about ten feet off the ground. Since your entrance route is your escape route, we're going to need the help of your trusty grappling hook and rope to climb back up. Attach one of the flukes of your grappling hook to something sturdy inside the vent you are in; it needs to withstand your weight. Footholds are also important here. You can find more information on crafting and using a grappling hook in Part I.

EXPLOITING THE SMITHSONIAN'S COMPUTERIZED SECURITY SYSTEM

Don't get ahead of yourself here. Before you go for the diamond, you'll need to take care of security. Before you can prompt the Hope Diamond's display case (and vault) to unlock, you need to trick the security system into *thinking* the museum is open. To do this you'll have to exploit the museum's computer system, which manages lighting, surveillance cameras, outer perimeter locks, and other automated systems. The terminal is always on and when given the correct user credentials, it will give you access to nearly everything.

The closest terminal is on the north wall of Geology Hall and is labeled *Security*. You will need to pick this lock, which should be relatively easy as it is a standard pin and tumbler lock (see page 11 for more details on lock picking). Here you will find a computer terminal not unlike your typical personal computer. It runs a commercial software and is secured by a username and password. Unfortunately, you're missing details pertinent to hacking the system, like user credentials and the operating system the computer runs on.

To get around this, you will set up a recording device to gather information and will return the *following* day to retrieve it. While this might seem extremely risky (breaking into the Smithsonian *twice*), remember how easy getting here really was: There are no walls or fencing to penetrate, the grounds are big and therefore undersurveyed, and finally, with simple tools and a ducting map, security is basically a nonissue. What you are doing here today is installing a GoPro portable camera outfitted with a third-party motion sensor (this will preserve battery life and storage space) to capture login information for your *future* use. To do this, attach the motion sensor to your GoPro and use your folding step stool to reach the ceiling. Use a lump of modeling clay to hold the camera in position and angle it to capture keystrokes on the terminal keyboard below. Make sure to double-check the angle so there are no obstructions.

You're done (for now). Take a quick survey to ensure everything is as you've left it. Close the door behind you. Use the rope ladder you've conveniently left for yourself to reenter the main air duct. Pull up the rope and slide the panel back shut. Traverse the ducts by following your map in reverse. Exit the geothermal heating unit and replace the panel. Once you are in the open, find your moped and keep a wary eye out as you drive back to your safe house. If all has gone to plan there should be more than enough time to escape unnoticed.

THE FOLLOW-UP

You don't want to wait long before making your reappearance. This particular system requires users to create new passwords every week, and even with the help of the motion-sensor attachment, the batteries on your GoPro won't last long. I recommend coming back within one to two days to avoid capturing login credentials that have since expired.

You're coming back the same way as before. You may be asking yourself, "What about my face—has it been captured on record?" Sure, on a digital drive *somewhere*. But in all likelihood no one has seen it. There simply aren't enough staff to review video from every camera and for every minute of the day. Assuming you did nothing wrong—no alarms were tripped, nothing reported as missing, and everything left as it was—the videos will *not* be reviewed.

Once you're through the maze of ducts, back down into the Geology Hall, and through the security door; remove the GoPro from the ceiling (yes, you will need your step stool) and review the video. This should be relatively easy thanks to your motion-sensor attachment, which has ensured only the action has been recorded.

Watch for a staff member who has logged into the console; this is where you will obtain your access code. Given the correct angle, you should have enough resolution to zoom in and see the keys clearly. You have at least *three* attempts at getting the username/password combination correct. Try not to blow it or you're looking at a narrow (and diamond-less) escape.

Once you have logged into the system, the interface should be intuitive. Find the *security cameras* interface and take a quick peek at the CCTV (closed-circuit television) feeds to ensure guards have not become aware of your presence. If all looks normal, navigate to the *scheduling* interface; here you will be able to alter the museums hours of operation. Remember, once you save your changes, get ready to act *fast*. The interior of the entire museum is about to light up like a shopping mall. Once this happens you will have only a few *minutes* to get the Hope Diamond and escape.

You may want to take some time to ponder the Hope Diamond's lurid past. For instance, Louis XIV, the Sun King of France, who purchased the diamond, later perished of gangrene. Louis XVI, who inherited the diamond, literally lost his head during the French Revolution. In 1910, the wealthy Evalyn Walsh McLean purchased the diamond from Pierre Cartier. Her mother-in-law died shortly thereafter; her first-born son died in an auto accident at the age of nine; her husband ran off with another woman; and her only daughter died of a drug overdose at the age of twenty-five. Evalyn died soon after her daughter's death. The list goes on.

Depending on what you believe, you may or may not be sitting by the flickering lights of the museum's computer terminal wondering if you too will soon be added to the Hope Diamond's long list of unfortunate owners. Will you be maimed like Princess de Lamballe? Hanged like Kulub Bey? Shamed like Lord Francis Hope, who was left old, without a family, and in financial ruin? Or will you enjoy the wealth, longevity, and happiness as the blue diamond's new hopeful holder?

GRAB AND GO

The Natural History Museum is now open for business, which means the Hope Diamond's display case has erected itself, thereby opening up your target for the taking. The chance that this tripped a silent alarm is extremely likely, and if not, any security guard within eyesight of the northwest wing will phone the breach in immediately. Remember: Opening the museum also means that the perimeter doors are unlocked, allowing you access to your moped within forty-five seconds.

The case protecting the Hope Diamond is not meant to withstand much force, which is why two guards are assigned to watch over the Hope Diamond during the hours the museum is open to the public. The guards are responsible for protecting the vulnerable diamond when it is unsheathed, and should the diamond become threatened in any way, they are responsible for subduing the threat. At this hour, with no visitors and no staff, there will be no one to stop you. But time is running out—so act fast.

Make your way over to the pedestal. It should require only a moderate blow of force—a strong kick will do—to knock the glass encasement, diamond and all, off the pedestal and onto the floor. The minute this happens alarms will begin to blare. Snatch up the diamond (don't worry about it breaking, diamond is one of the hardest elements we know of) and head back to and up your trusty rope ladder. Leave the ladder behind this time, and exit back through the duct system. Find your moped and take to the side streets, the darker the better. You have less than *five* minutes to get back to your safe house.

> If you're wondering why you're not simply exiting through a door, the answer is simple: Entrances and exits will be the first thing secured once authorities arrive. By the time someone thinks to check the air-conditioning unit, you will be safe in your motel room.

BEDDING DOWN

During the preheist planning period you will have stocked your hideaway with enough food, drinks, and entertainment to last you two to three weeks, roughly the length of time a heist of this scale will keep the attention of the city officials. The search will consist of an initial sweep of the area with on-ground patrol, helicopters, checkpoints, and heightened airport and border security. Following the two- to three-week period, investigation protocol will relegate the case to desk detectives, a safe time to securely make your escape out of Washington, DC.

Reserve a rental car online under your false identity; you want something generic. You want to do nothing to call attention to yourself; minimal face time is, as always, critical. Interstate 270 is your best bet: a straight shot west, and away from the densely populated east—toward freedom.

True freedom, of course, has no borders. Freedom is won slowly, meticulously. No matter how fast you push the engine of your rented escape vehicle, the key to your freedom is *patience*. So take it slow and enjoy dreaming about your new life, the life that's yours once you're able to liquidate your priceless gem into cold, hard cash. But bear in mind: There is a long and dark history of those who have possessed the blue Hope Diamond before you. You never know what lies ahead.

THE *MONA LISA*

APPROXIMATE VALUE
$760 million

LOCATION
The Louvre, Paris, France

EQUIPMENT REQUIRED
Nondescript sedan (2)
Steel crowbar
Lightweight laptop
Sunglasses
Beret or baseball cap

ABOUT THE *MONA LISA*

The *Mona Lisa*, a half-length portrait of a woman by the Italian artist Leonardo da Vinci, is acclaimed by John Lichfield as "the best known, the most visited, the most written about, the most sung about, and the most parodied work of art in the world." The painting is thought to be a portrait of Lisa Gherardini, the wife of a successful silk merchant, and was painted circa 1503. It is now the property of the French Republic, on permanent display at the Louvre museum in Paris.

In 1962, the painting was assessed for insurance at $100,000,000. However, once adjusted for inflation, the iconic painting is worth somewhere to the tune of $760,000,000, making it one of the most (if not *the* most) valuable paintings in the world.

OVERVIEW

When the *Mona Lisa* disappeared from the Louvre in 1911, the world was shocked. How could a heist so simple and with only a single individual involved actually succeed? Well, it *nearly* did. To make this work you need a comprehensive understanding of the security cameras in the Salle des Etats and a janitorial position at the Louvre itself. And, finally, you will need to create a grand distraction worthy of diverting the eyes of Paris just long enough for you to stroll out the front entrance, painting in tow, and vanish into the streets unseen.

PREPARATION

Your starting point will be the modest, yet ingenious, footsteps of Vincenzo Peruggia—a former employee of the Louvre, and a thief. Using his firsthand familiarity with the museum's security—or lack thereof—Peruggia knew that the easiest way to pull off what would become one of the most famous art heists in history was to literally walk out the front door. And so he did.

Peruggia's simple plan went something like this:

1. He disguised himself as a museum worker.
2. He hid out inside the museum until after closing hours.
3. He slipped by the after-hours staff.
4. He pried the painting off the wall with a crowbar.
5. He took the painting to a deserted stairwell.
6. He removed the bulky protective casing.
7. He slipped the painting under a smock he wore.
8. And, finally, he walked out the front door.

> Vincenzo Peruggia was ultimately caught due to a faulty assumption; he was attempting to return the painting to Italy, where he believed it belonged. He was promptly turned in and arrested.

But let's not get ahead of ourselves. It was 1911 when Vincenzo Peruggia passed casually by an unsuspecting guard and out of the Louvre's main entrance. There are fewer exits in today's Louvre as well as updated state-of-the-art security systems that monitor each collection closely. This includes hundreds of cameras strategically placed in each of the museums "districts," which are also monitored 24/7 by security personnel.

Seemingly impossible-to-penetrate security standards aside, you need to start somewhere, and that somewhere is a job application for a custodial position at the Louvre. This will get you access that would be otherwise impossible to attain.

> Janitorial positions see a lot of turnover, so I expect this position will be open reliably. If you can't find an open position, keep an eye out until you do. About 90 percent of the game here is patience—it's what separates the people who wind up in prison and *you*.

If the responsibilities of your new position are unclear, expect something like this:

> **Duties of a Museum Custodian:** Reports to the Custodian Lead, who is responsible for the direction of housekeeping services in the facility. Clean and sanitize restrooms. Clean, dust, and care for displays; sweep, mop, and vacuum floors; empty wastebaskets and trash containers; replace light bulbs; refill restroom dispensers; etc.

There are three reasons you need to obtain this particular position:

> You will be given keys to all floors, galleries, and offices.
>
> You will learn the nuances of the museum's security system.
>
> You will become a trusted and familiar face to museum staff and security.

Custodial positions at the Louvre are easy to secure and do not require references. Visit the "Louvre Careers" section of their website (louvregroup.com /careers) and download an application. Fill it out and wait. This kind of planning takes time, so be patient.

YOUR NEW JOB AT THE LOUVRE

Congratulations, you're hired! The first day on any job is always exciting, and your new custodial position at the Louvre is no exception. Your goal is to maintain this position for at least a few months. This means you must be punctual and take your janitorial duties seriously. You want to be familiar but forgettable.

While others may consider your days dull and repetitious, you will actually be hard at work educating yourself on three primary aspects of the museum:

1. **Security**
   a. Location of computer terminals.
   b. Position and coverage of security cameras.
   c. Exploitable nuances of museum security.
2. **Floor plan**
   a. Quickest routes to all exits—most important, the Porte des Lions exit (from which you will escape).
   b. Traffic patterns of museumgoers in and around the Salle des Etats gallery (know where bottlenecks occur and in which directions visitor traffic flows).
3. **The *Mona Lisa***
   a. Observing and notating the painting's mounting apparatus.
   b. Noting "blackout dates," when the painting might be closed to the public.

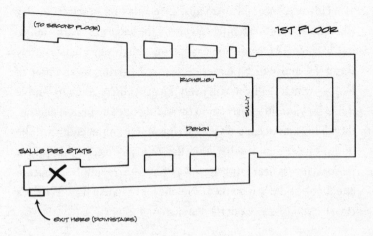

This information, coupled with the details laid out in the remainder of this chapter, will be enough to pull off one of the most newsworthy heists in this book; a ubiquitously studied masterpiece, Leonardo da Vinci's enigmatic opus, the most visited painting on Earth. And it will be *yours*.

THE PLAN

It's been several months since you started working at the Louvre, and as far as everyone is concerned, you are now part of the team. Your next move is to plan a distraction that will divert the attention of anyone in the immediate area away from the Louvre, the *Mona Lisa*—and most important, *you*. It must be a distraction that will absorb the National Gendarmerie (France's police force) and draw as many art enthusiasts as possible *out* of the most highly trafficked museum in Paris. But remember: *prudence over violence*.

How are you going to do this? By employing an actress to play a hopeless soul-threatening suicide on the ledge of a nearby building, of course. Morbid? Some might say. But this incident is purely theatrical and will be exposed as a red herring in a matter of hours—which is all you will need. Finally, you're going to double down on your little distraction by adding one key ingredient: nudity. This may seem a bit garish to you, but in the end it will be nothing more than another show for our female lead as this kind of performance is her nightly business. She is there simply to capture attention. And where to find someone for a job like this? Well, it's time for you to check out the Parisian nightlife.

CASTING YOUR LEAD ROLE

Clearly, you will need to find a woman comfortable with being naked in an extremely public setting. The best place to find such a person would be in the Quartier Rouge (the red light district), which is on Rue Saint-Denis and is one of the oldest regions of Paris. It's easy to locate: The road runs between Boulevard de Bonne-Nouvelle and Rue de Rivoli. Here you will find several adult shops and what in America are called "gentlemen's clubs" (although there doesn't seem to be much that is gentlemanly about them). Club 199 is a good place to start and you must do so in disguise so you won't be recognized when this is all over. Order a drink and when you spot a dancer who looks the part, offer her a hefty tip and invite her to sit down and talk with you. Of course, she will think you are going to make an arrangement for some after-hours pleasure. Let her think that; you do not want to discuss your plan in a public place.

There will be situations, like this one, where following steps simply won't suffice. There is a kind of *savoir-faire* required to close a deal like this. Do you have the social skills and confidence to pull it off? Only you know the answer, and if not, it would be best to move on to a more suitable campaign.

Once trust has been established, take your new friend for a walk along the Seine—a commercial waterway south of the Louvre that runs east to west; find an empty bench with no one around. Sit down and tell her only what she needs to know (she does not need to know you are planning to steal the *Mona Lisa*; as a Parisian, she may object). Tell her that you need someone to create a distraction by threatening to jump off the roof of the Cafe Tabac building, kitty corner to the Louvre, at precisely 12 noon on a date yet to be determined, and that she must be completely naked when she threatens to do so. She must continue the ruse for at least thirty minutes before she allows a gendarme to help her down. For her services, you will pay her €5,000; half out front, and the remainder, if she has done her job well, to be paid at Club 199 two days later. Considering the salaries of pole dancers, she will, in all likelihood, jump at the chance. If not, you simply move on to the next person or the next heist (depending on how much you've been exposed).

SECURITY AT THE LOUVRE

While security at the Louvre has vastly improved since 1911, you won't find yourself navigating a crisscrossing laser-beam detector or having to warm the galleries to avoid body heat detection or any other outlandish Hollywood-type feats. The Louvre today uses your classic bread-and-butter security practices to keep its trove of priceless collectables safe.

Don't let all of the security rattle you too much. There have been several before you that have taken a bite out of the grinning *Mona Lisa*.

For instance, in April 1974, a woman upset by the museum's policy for disabled people sprayed red paint across the $50,000 Triplex glass case while the painting was on display at the Tokyo National Museum. In August 2009, a Russian woman, distraught over being denied French citizenship, threw a terra-cotta mug, purchased at the museum's gift shop, at the painting.

The important thing to note here is that in both cases it took five to ten minutes before any personnel showed up on the scene. Let this sink in: You will have time, so long as you act fast and stay calm.

Surveillance Systems

When designing surveillance for the Louvre, security experts were tasked with figuring out how to get the most coverage using the fewest number of cameras. This was done as a cost-saving measure (video feeds need to be monitored, which requires personnel) and so it provides an opportunity for you: Small blind spots exist throughout the museum where the vertices of the cameras' focal points do not completely intersect, thereby creating a *hole*. In some cases these holes were created as new structural features were added to the interior of the Louvre.

Let's take, for instance, the various remodels of the Salle des Etats that over the years have added features such as higher ceilings, semicircular arcades, marble paneling, and most important, a slight inset of the east wall—behind which someone can hide without being seen by any of the gallery's *three* cameras.

Security Personnel

In addition to cameras, there are the men and women with access to alarm systems, the National Gendarmerie, and of course, weapons. These are the people you must avoid altogether. Make a wrong turn and you could wind up staring down the barrel of a SIG Sauer.

FINDING YOUR PARTNER

As discussed, you will take on the lion's share of the risk in this campaign, which involves prying the *Mona Lisa* off the wall, getting out of the building, and switching vehicles at the predetermined change point. But unlike Vincenzo Peruggia, you need a reliable and trustworthy individual who you are confident can partner on a job of this scale (and who you can trust will not double-cross you).

Partner (At a 25 Percent Take)

Here's exactly what your partner will responsible for:

1. Securing two getaway vehicles.
   a. A nondescript sedan.
   b. A *switch car* (also a nondescript sedan), which will be parked across the Seine and used as a precaution against exterior cameras.
2. Making the anonymous call to the National Gendarmerie at precisely 12:05 p.m. on the date of the heist to report a woman about to jump off the rooftop of Cafe Tabac.

THE PLAN

You have been working alongside museum staff as a janitor for several months now. People know you. You're friendly, quiet, but always reliable. If asked about you, one would say something along the lines of, "So-and-so is a hard worker and a good person. There's no way he [or she] had anything to do with this." This is the kind of reaction you want from people when questioned by police.

When the time comes to pry the *Mona Lisa* off of the wall you will need an appropriate tool: a conveniently hidden crowbar. While this step may seem relatively simple (get a crowbar into the museum, unseen), there is more to it than just strolling into work one day with a crowbar in your trousers.

Every time you enter the museum you will be required to pass through security. This is where your knowledge of the security patterns and, more important, weaknesses, will come into play. These are the details no book could ever claim to contain. Any security system installed to protect thirty-five thousand objects dating from prehistory to the twenty-first century, exhibited in a 230,000-square-foot space, will perforce have some holes in it: The security guard who takes an extra ten minutes on his or her lunch break, the door that is supposed to be locked but never is, the faulty metal detector that hasn't picked up the keys you've *purposely* left in your pocket. In a facility visited by eight million people every year, there is bound to be a way of slipping in a 2.5-pound steel crowbar. It's up to you to find it.

> Once the crowbar is in the museum all you need to do is hide it out of sight and relatively close to the Salle des Etats, so it is easily accessible by you. As long as the crowbar is hidden from guests, it should go unnoticed and remain unmoved by staff. Given your privileged access, the right location should be relatively easy to find.

You will also need to prepare two separate getaway cars. One of these cars will be used by your partner to retrieve you (and the painting) from the museum entrance. The other will be a switch car, which you will use in case the car you were picked up in is captured on closed circuit television (CCTV). You must make sure there is no video record of the car that you use to leave the country.

Find two midsize sedans with decent size trunks (while the painting is surprisingly small, the encasement is quite large and bulky), capable of speeds up to two hundred kilometers per hour, gas tanks full. Make sure they are dissimilar in make and color. Park one of the cars across the Seine where you can easily find it and in a location with ample parking. Since you will abandon your first car the last thing you need is to be looking for a parking space when half of the National Gendarmerie is searching for you.

THE TIME LINE
You should have all the pieces in place now. On the day of the heist, the order of events should proceed as outlined.

8:45 a.m.
You go to work just as usual, nothing changes. Keep in mind your face has been captured on digital hard drives for months now. You don't want any suspicion to be drawn your way when security footage is reviewed, which it will many times over once the *Mona Lisa* has gone missing.

12:00 p.m.
At noon, a naked woman will begin screaming from the rooftop. The Place du Carrousel will be packed with people on their lunch break at this time, which will serve to amplify disorder and draw more of the Lou-

vre's security to Cour Carrée et Pyramide du Louvre and as far away from the *Mona Lisa*—and you—as possible.

12:05 p.m.

At 12:05, your partner will make a telephone call to the local police station from a payphone nearby. He will tell the police that a woman is about to jump off the roof of the building at 2 Rue de l'Amiral de Coligny. (Of course, it is entirely possible that the police have already received numerous calls from the cell phones of those gathered in the Place du Carrousel; this is just a precaution to ensure the phone call takes place.) Once the information is received, he should hang up and immediately flee the scene.

12:06 p.m.

Find the nearest fire alarm that is sufficiently masked from cameras (you should already have it identified) and pull it. As you do this you want to elevate the chaos by screaming out, "There's a naked suicide jumper in Cour Carrée!" Make sure to keep your head turned down and away from any cameras. If well-orchestrated, the combination of a rooftop jumper, the triggered alarm, and your call of distress should be enough to light the match of panic and send people running to catch a glimpse; which is exactly what you want.

12:10 p.m.

Get to the Salle des Etats where the painting resides and wait. You should be close to the east wall with the marble inset—this is the blind spot you're going to exploit. Soon sirens will be heard as les gendarmeries arrive from various quarters to aid the jumper. There will be a few moments of confusion as both patrons and Louvre security try to figure out what's going on. When a calamitous event like this occurs news travels from person to person rapidly. The gawker mentality can always be relied on—people will begin to rush out of the museum to spectate.

Once this happens and the Salle des Etats is jammed with people trying to exit, your goal is to wedge your body into the inset. The difficult part will be tim-

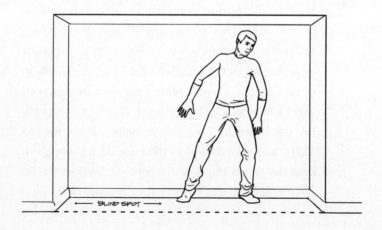

←— BLIND SPOT —→

ing. You want to use the confusion to mask yourself as you vanish into the camera's blind spot. When this footage is reviewed you want to be lost in the crowd as the museumgoers pour out of the east exit. Once you are there, tucked away from view, all you have to do is wait.

12:17 p.m.
It will take one to two minutes for the Louvre's internal emergency system to fully kick in; the system was deliberately designed with a delay to give administrators time to retract in case of a false alarm. You will know the system has fully kicked in when the power in the building cuts off and is replaced with flashing strobe lights and a blaring alarm. Don't worry though, this is a good thing.

The flashing strobes ensure that the cameras will be unable to pick up your face, allowing you to leave your hideout to go retrieve the crowbar. Do it with haste.

12:20 p.m.
Once you return you want to get to work on the painting immediately. The *Mona Lisa* is not designed to withstand much force, and with a few good heaves you should be able to pry off the braces and remove it from the wall. Bear in mind this encasement is extremely heavy, somewhere between twenty and thirty pounds. The *Mona Lisa* is painted on wood paneling and should withstand moderate jostling, but be careful, finding a restoration artist to work on a stolen piece of art from

the sixteenth century could add years to the process of turning this piece over.

 12:25 p.m.
Remove the painting from the back paneling by using the flat end of the crowbar. Remember, it will be difficult to see you with the lights off and strobes flashing. This will take some time, but remember this is why we've created such a dramatic distraction: to give you the time and cover you need to get the painting out safely. Once you're done, throw on a pair of dark sunglasses and a cap for additional cover as you prepare to leave. You should be able to pass freely through the museum's south wing, through the guard station, and to your first getaway car, which, if your partner has done his part, should be waiting directly out front.

It's important at this step that you keep your head down and eyes toward the street. There are over a dozen outdoor security cameras capturing the faces of people entering the Louvre, so don't look back. The National Gendarmerie will still be in the process of locking down the area, but if timed right, you should be able to get out before barricades and checkpoints have been put in place.

 12:26 p.m.
Your partner should be right out front. There is no parking here. But if your timing is right, this should be

a smooth pickup. Quickly pack the painting securely into the trunk, get in the passenger side, and go.

12:27 p.m.
You want to head east toward the Pont Neuf Bridge, away from the Pompidou Center, where everything is happening. Keep your speed under control as you cross over the water and find your switch vehicle. Park your car, grab the painting from the back, get it into the trunk of your new ride, and head south toward the network of highways that surround Paris. Take the first connection to the E50 you can find. Once you're out of the immediate area, you're home free.

You're going to want to hide the painting someplace where it will be safe for several months. A rented apartment should work (procured with cash and under a fake name, as usual), as long as you aren't living there. It should be at least ten miles away from your actual dwelling and the Louvre itself. Once you tuck away your treasure, keep driving for at least ten more miles and leave your car there. Take a train, bus, or taxi back home and stay there for the remainder of the day. Turn on the TV and relax. It's been a long three months, and it's not over yet.

THE AFTERMATH

Assuming you did everything correctly, your involvement with the theft should stay a secret—you made sure your presence was shielded from cameras, thereby erasing the link between you and the *Mona Lisa* during the time of the theft. Go back to work the following day, as usual, to cement your innocence. You will likely be questioned intensely, as will all museum personnel. Keep your story simple: "I heard an alarm. Everyone started running, so I ran. Once I saw the woman on the roof, I felt ill, so I took a train home." No reason to elaborate more than that.

Play it cool and continue to show up for work. Make sure to return to Club 199 to pay off the dancer the following day. She needs to continue to keep cool—she has most likely associated you with the crime. This is fine, as long as she doesn't know your name or your face (assuming your face has been sufficiently disguised). Stay on the job for another few months. Then you can quit, citing your grandmother's poor health, which requires you to return to wherever you are from immediately.

As you fly home with a package worth over $100,000,000 tucked in the overhead compartment (don't worry, paintings aren't illegal to travel with and cannot be discerned via X-ray), you will most certainly begin to daydream about your future. An enigmatic smile might creep onto your face. Your friends and colleagues will notice, they will wonder where this mysterious smile of yours comes from; they will wonder, but they will never really know. And you, you will just keep smiling.

ARCHAEOPTERYX LITHOGRAPHICA

APPROXIMATE VALUE
$5 million

LOCATION
Museum für Naturkunde, Berlin, Germany

EQUIPMENT REQUIRED
Handheld magnetometer
Handheld GPS device
Fluxgate compass
110-volt industrial electromagnet
9-mm video scope inspection camera
CB500-HH handheld pneumatic core drill
2,000 rpm concrete flat-saw
Flat-saw blades (40)
Shovels (2)
Pickaxes (2)
Short sledgehammer
2,500-watt gasoline generator
115-volt inline duct fan for 8-inch duct
Dolly
100 feet of 6-inch flexible ducting
80 feet of industrial power cabling
200-watt work lights (20)
Folding stepladder
2-foot, 4×4 posts (95+)
Hard hat
Iron wedge

Crowbar
Musician's tour cases (5)
Death metal album
Ski mask

ABOUT THE *ARCHAEOPTERYX LITHOGRAPHICA*

In 1859, Charles Darwin unlocked our understanding of our origins with his theory of natural selection, documented in his most revered and recognized work, *On the Origin of Species*. Despite overwhelming evidence that supports the theory's veracity, there are still some that refute the notion that Earth is so many magnitudes older than what is depicted in the Bible.

Early on, one of the more powerful arguments against Darwin's radical new theory was the absence of a specific type of fossil called a *linking fossil*. Linking fossils are physical records that show a transition, or evolution, from one species to another. Darwin's theory inferred that if species did evolve, they would be left behind as part of the fossil record—but so far none had been found.

It wasn't until 1861, two years later, when *Archaeopteryx* was discovered in the Solnhofen limestone, located in southern Germany. *Archaeopteryx* was immediately celebrated by scientists as it captured in startling detail something never before seen in a Late Jurassic Period specimen: feathers. It was this feathered creature that became the first direct evidence of an intermediate species—one that inextricably linked dinosaurs to modern-day birds. It is for this reason some consider *Archaeopteryx litho-*

graphica one of the world's most important and valuable fossils ever discovered.

OVERVIEW

Established in 1810, the Naturkunde is one of the largest museums in all of Germany and contains over ten thousand specimens. To protect this priceless catalog, including the largest mounted dinosaur in the world, the Naturkunde is built like a fortress, and during business hours employs around twenty armed security guards. In addition to armed personnel, the museum employs a state-of-the-art security system consisting of CCTV, motion sensors, and gallery vaults to keep the museum galleries and grounds secure. Set in a dense urban area, the museum is surrounded by a network of high-traffic streets, making an undetected escape nearly impossible.

To sidestep insurmountable odds and almost certain capture we will be employing a tactic of Hollywood proportions; a dangerous endeavor through the ground to infiltrate the Naturkunde by exploiting its most vulnerable point: the foundation. There is perhaps nothing more romantic in the world of high-stakes thievery than tunneling below ground to acquire the impossible. Come to see the largest fossilized *Brachiosaurus* in the world, a towering prehistoric skeleton, but leave with a priceless lithographic limestone of a bird that has challenged how we think about our own origins. It's time to get your hard hat and pickax ready.

PREPARATION

With such a long equipment list, you're going to want to be smart about how and where you make your purchases. Certain shopping patterns may raise red flags for anyone who might be snooping your Internet traffic or monitoring your bank activity. Therefore, you want to avoid shopping for equipment online or using credit cards. These purchases need to be made in person, not over the Internet. Take note of the plurality: *purchases*. It may seem excessive, but the prudent thing to do is to spread your procurements across multiple stores. Also, you're going to make your purchases in cash, so you need a hefty amount of upfront capital to fund your little project.

A DISGUISE YOU CAN LIVE IN

Just like any job in this book, the *Archaeopteryx lithographica* requires early planning. Due to the density of video surveillance in the regions surrounding the museum, I'm recommending you take on a false identity. Once you have made the decision to move forward you should have ample time to create a disguise you can comfortably slip in and out of for months on end.

Wigs are a great way to change your look completely without a lot of work. Clothing and accessories are also excellent tools to enhance the look of your character. You want to look uninteresting but at the same time you want to be able to dramatically change your appearance at a moment's notice. When the job is done you will lose the wig, cut or dye your hair, shave your beard, toss away spectacles, change your clothes—whatever you can do quickly and easily so you can walk out of the area without being recognized. But during the preheist period, you will wear your new disguise any time you are out in public. No exceptions. Berlin is littered with cameras and you need to make sure your real identity is not picked up by any of them.

YOUR NEW RESIDENCE
Once your equipment checklist is taken care of you should be ready to switch gears and start looking for your temporary residence in Berlin. This is going to be your base of operations for the next three months. The buildings you are targeting are located directly west of the Naturkunde on Invalidenstraße, roughly 160 feet away from the museum (see map on page 75). You will be going through the entire rental process in character, using one of your forged identities. Don't worry if your German is poor, you can use this to your advantage by playing the part of a relocated foreigner who can't speak a word. Sometimes playing dumb is the smartest thing a thief can do.

COME ON FEEL THE NOISE
At this point you might be thinking to yourself, *I see where this is going, but what about the noise? Won't tunneling through the floorboards and under the building of a busy apartment complex be a little loud?* The short answer is yes; you will need a plan to mask the disturbance. Your cover is going to be a rock band, of which you are a member. And your band is going to be loud—*really* loud.

Find an obscure death metal album brash enough to drown out heavy construction. While you may get complaints from the neighbors, they certainly won't suspect what is *really* happen-

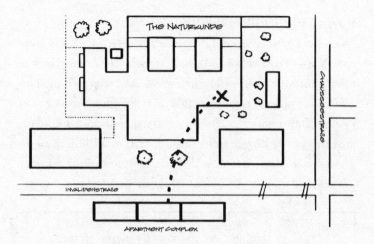

ing. Any complaints you do get should take several months to turn into a court-mandated eviction. So don't worry, by the time your landlord comes with papers in hand you'll be relaxing on a private beach, enjoying a martini.

You're going to need to hide more than just the sound though. At one of the many music shops in Berlin you will find tour cases for traveling bands. These are large, heavy-duty cases for transporting bulky touring equipment, such as amps and instruments. They will allow you to bring equipment in and excavated material out, while at the same time bolstering your story as a rock musician.

> In all likelihood, your neighbors will be too aggravated by the noise to notice your nonexistent bandmates.

HOW TO TUNNEL UNDERGROUND

There's no getting around it—tunneling underground is going to be a feat of hard labor and steadfast patience. You will be burrowing through layers of flooring, wood, concrete, soil, and bedrock. This process is going to take anywhere from two to three months and is going to require rigorous, nonstop work. If you are ready and willing to suffer through drilling a 160-foot underground tunnel, the result will be an easy-in/easy-out museum job that will make you $5,000,000 richer, overnight.

Before starting, you need to be aware of the legal consequences of tunneling underground. If anyone finds out about this little project of yours, you will most likely be locked up immediately. Tunneling is legal only on private property (that you own) and never under a property border. Since you will be breaking *both* of these laws, discretion is absolutely paramount.

To start off, measure out and cut a three-foot square hole into the floor using your electric flat saw. Keep your lights off to avoid a power surge, but also to keep curious eyes from catching peeks through your windows. At first the drilling will be loud, while you cut through the flooring layers as well as the core and stabilizing layers. Keep blasting your music to mask the sound. Progress will be slow but keep in mind;

you're going for a low profile until you have enough earth between you and your apartment to absorb the sound of the heavier drilling. The cut should be roughly four feet deep to get through the top layers of flooring, baseboards, and the concrete foundation slab (see the illustration on page 86). Your flat saw should be able to get through all of this with ease, including any reinforcing rod. Expect to go through a new sawblade for every four inches you dig.

Once you have your frame cut out, the interior can be excavated using a four-inch iron wedge and short sledgehammer. Fill the empty tour cases with the excavated material. Remove the cases (before they're too heavy to lift) using a dolly, load them into a truck, and find a discreet location to dispose of them. This is best done late at night while making sure no one is watching.

Understanding the Soil Profile

Once you have made it through the concrete foundation you should hit pay dirt—which in this case is literally *dirt*. Let's go over the soil profile and what it will take to get through each layer:

[R] Surface soil: Mineral soil depleted of iron, clay, aluminum, and organic compounds. This layer should be relatively easy to penetrate using shovels and pickaxes. Dig time: one to two days.

[F] Subsoil: Iron, clay, and aluminum. Dig time will slow down significantly. Your shovel will no longer work at this

LAYERS & SOIL TYPES

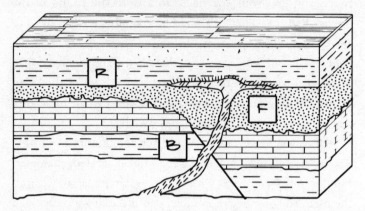

point. Use your pickax here and make sure to maintain a three-by-three-foot frame. Dig time: three to five days.

[B] Parent rock: Larger rocks and hardened earth. While this layer is distinctively different from the subsoil, it should have little effect on your dig time. Continue with your pickax, shoring off and excavating large chunks at a time. Dig time: five to seven days.

Once you are roughly ten feet deep, you should be through your surface soil [R], subsoil [F], and one to two feet into bedrock [B]—this is the farthest down you will have to dig before the second leg of your journey which will take you under Invalidenstraße and directly toward your target—the *Archaeopteryx lithographica*.

It's possible, should you not think ahead, to dig yourself into a hole you can't climb out of. And with music blasting, your neighbors may never hear your screams for help. For this reason you should keep a folding stepladder with you once the hole is no longer easy to climb out of.

WHICH WAY IS WHICH?

The exact coordinates of the *Archaeopteryx lithographica*'s vault room are +52°31'52.50", +13°22'46.14". These numbers are important, as you need to come up directly beneath the vault in which the target is kept. While it might seem as simple as plugging the coordinates into a GPS device and tunneling to your destination, there's a critical drawback that you probably haven't considered—GPS requires an unobstructed line of sight between your device and the sky and therefore will not work.

A magnetometer is a device that operates much like a traditional compass with one key distinction—it works in *three* dimensions. This special compass can be used to measure your location in proximity to a magnetic source, which in your case will communicate your dig position above ground where your latitude and longitude can be measured via GPS. You're going to want to check your position roughly every twenty feet you dig to make sure you're headed in the right direction, toward the precise coordinates of the *Archaeopteryx*. To do this, place a 110-volt (or greater) industrial electromagnet inside your tunnel, at the farthest point

HOW TO STEAL THE MONA LISA

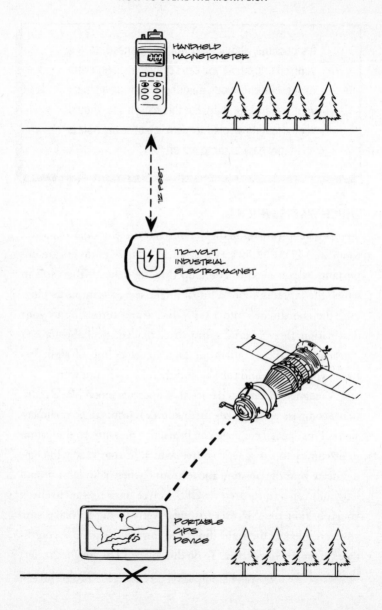

you've dug. This will generate a strong magnetic field that, once you're back above ground, you can measure, using your magnetometer, to locate your tunneling position. You should be able to make your measurements discreetly as you move outside of the apartment complex, across Invalidenstraße, into the grounds of the museum, and finally inside the museum itself.

The process of tracking your dig position goes as follows:

1. Using your fluxgate compass, dig in the direction of the target for roughly twenty feet.

2. Place your super magnet at the farthest end of your tunnel.

3. Leave the tunnel and find your dig position using your magnetometer.

4. Standing where you are, use your GPS device to retrieve your latitude and longitude.

5. Calculate the distance and direction using your current position and the position of the target (+52°31'52.50", +13°22'46.14").

6. Crawl back down through the tunnel; remove the magnet, and using your fluxgate compass, correct for any errors in your dig trajectory.

7. Repeat.

While GPS can be difficult to use indoors you should have access to enough windows inside the Naturkunde to retrieve your coordinates accurately.

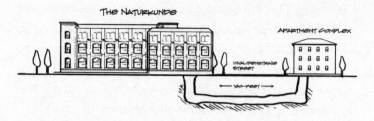

You are digging an elongated U shape with ten-foot-deep access points and a connecting passage of roughly 160 feet in length (of course, this depends on where you found your rental unit). The main length of your tunnel needs to be only three feet in diameter. The smaller the channel, the quicker and safer your dig will be.

This is where the real work comes into play, most of which will be done with your CB500-HH handheld pneumatic core drill. This is a specialized tool and so we will not be able to detail how to operate the drill here. However, there should be enough documentation that comes with the machine to get you started on the heavier, horizontal excavation.

A SAFE TUNNEL YOU CAN WORK IN

Along with the legal risks there are potential safety threats as well, including being struck by dangerous machinery, being buried alive by cave-ins, and being drowned by accidentally tapping into a high-pressure water main. While most of these dangers are difficult to protect against, cave-ins are the most common, yet most avoidable, risk you will face in underground tunneling.

Subterranean lateral support must be integrated as you dig to compensate for the weakness you are introducing through excavation. In order to remain stable, tunnels must be able to withstand the loads placed on them. *Dead load* is a term that refers to the weight of the structure itself, while *live load* refers to your own weight as you move through the tunnel. The dead and live loads you are dealing with can be countered by installing four-by-four support beams as you dig, typically every five to ten feet.

In addition, you will need to install proper ventilation using your 2,500-watt gasoline generator, a fan, and roughly a hundred feet of six-inch ducting. The goal is to flush out the poisonous gasses inside the tunnel and pump fresh oxygen in from above. Extend the ducting as you bore farther in, and cut two-inch holes every ten feet or so to allow for an even distribution of fresh air.

> Both a hard hat and proper ventilation are absolutely critical once you are roughly ten feet deep. The vapors combined with the low oxygen levels can render you unconscious, thereby killing you without warning.

You're going to need power as well. Continue to extend your cable as you dig farther in, adding a work light at each power cord junction. Your 2,500-watt gasoline generator should provide enough juice to cover your drilling, lighting, and ventilation, for the entire dig. You can expect to refuel every four to six hours.

COMING UP IN THE WORLD

Tunneling under the foundation of a massive complex, through sedimentary rock, under sidewalks and busy streets, and beyond the boundaries of the highest security museum in Berlin, is no small feat. However, with steadfast determination and some good-old-fashioned elbow grease you should be there in eight to ten weeks.

> This is probably a good time to purchase your plane ticket out of Berlin and to wherever you plan to go next. Pick a date eight to ten weeks out and make sure you are departing in the early morning, between 2 and 7, from Berlin Tegel Airport (TXL).

Once you begin your journey back upward, you need to be careful to not block yourself in. Trips back to your apartment with buckets of rock and dirt will be numerous, and they will slow things down considerably. However, if you get lazy here, you will only be doubling your work by digging your way back out. You want to make sure you have enough room to traverse the length of your tunnel easily. It should take you no more than twenty minutes to travel from one end of the tunnel to the other.

Once you are directly under the gallery room, you can begin

your journey to the surface. Use the soil profile (see the diagram on page 78) to gauge how close you are to the museum's underbelly. When you hit the subsoil layer, stop. Due to the noise factor, you will be operating from 10 p.m. to 5 a.m. from this point forward, while the Naturkunde is empty. Even though you have switched back to your pickax and shovel there is still risk of someone in the museum picking up on suspicious vibrations from beneath their feet. As you work your way up to the surface soil layer you want to slow your pace considerably. Keep your upward channel constrained to a three-foot-square hole to protect against a cave-in. When you reach the underside of the museum's foundational block, you should stop again.

The next and last leg of your trip is going to take roughly four to six hours, which should be more than enough time to get you up through the foundational layers of the museum's west wing and into the gallery vault where the *Archaeopteryx* is kept. The last stretch must be accomplished before daylight.

Bear in mind, you still have to find your way out of Berlin before the museum opens, so you need to add additional time to collect your things and get to the airport. That means you need to have your bags packed—leaving nothing personally identifiable behind!

THE FINAL STRETCH

Before continuing your dig, you're going to need to check your position one last time to ensure you are directly under the west gallery room that houses the *Archaeopteryx*. Make sure you are in disguise when entering the museum as a guest. There are no bag checks at the Naturkunde, so you don't have to worry about bringing in your magnetometer and GPS devices—they are small enough to store on your person anyway. Make your way to the center of the *Archaeopteryx*'s gallery room and discreetly take your measurements. You will be using these data to position yourself exactly where you will be coming up through the floor. Once you have what you need, it's time to leave and head back to your apartment. Come 10 p.m. you will be making your final journey through the tunnel.

At 10, the Naturkunde will be completely empty. This time, bring your ski mask and video scope inspection camera. Make your way back through your tunnel and using your fluxgate

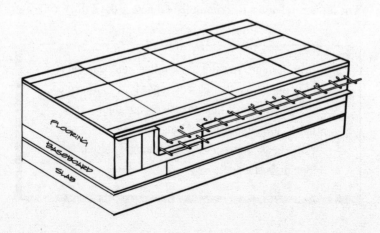

compass, magnetometer, and GPS, find your insertion point and mark it off on the underside of the foundational slab. Using your boring bit, start drilling until you get through the flooring, which is most likely eight to twelve inches thick. Now, feed your scope up through the hole you've drilled to survey your position. You want to be inside and within a few feet of the surrounding walls. If you need to reposition yourself, do so, but keep in mind that you have a flight to catch.

Once confident in your position, use your iron wedge and sledgehammer to crack away at the edges of your three-by-three-foot frame. You need to work quickly and steadily, keeping track of worrisome cracks that might be early signs of a cave-in. Once you've begun to break through the final layer, you're going to need to mask up. The Naturkunde is a highly secured museum with cameras monitoring every square inch, and you don't want to be wearing a wig and prosthetics while doing manual labor. And so, before you surface you want to make sure your face is covered completely—a ski mask will work just fine.

Alarms should not be a problem if you have calculated your position correctly. In the Naturkunde, there are no motion detectors inside the gallery vaults, so as long as you keep your face covered your presence there will be silent and untraceable.

> At this point you will know very quickly whether or not you have failed. If you've managed to somehow alert any unexpected guard staff you will probably find yourself staring down the barrel of a firearm.

THE ESCAPE

The *Archaeopteryx lithographica* is encased in two-inch-thick armored glass and bolted to an oak shelf that rolls in and out of an isolated vault for viewing. Getting the locked case open will prove to be difficult in the little time you have; pry the entire case, specimen and all, off of the shelf and deal with opening the case later. Don't worry; the shelf is not built to withstand much force. With a well-placed crowbar and a little elbow grease, you should be able to pop the hinges off and get to the limestone *Archaeopteryx*. The whole thing, case and all, is about 2.8 by 1.5 feet and weighs somewhere between twenty and thirty pounds.

Back down into the hole you go. You don't have much time before the museum opens and the entire area goes on lockdown. Make your way back home through your trusty tunnel. You need to be on the road and headed to TXL within thirty minutes. Clean yourself up, grab your bags and tickets, and hail a taxi. All of these things need to be ready and syncopated so you can get out of dodge with the *Archaeopteryx* tucked away in a suitcase before the first museum staff members arrive.

THE GETAWAY

All of the digging and hard labor has finally paid off—in the millions, in fact. As the taxi whisks you away, think of some pedagogic explanation to offer security should they question the odd item in your suitcase when it goes through X-ray. Perhaps you are a geologist bringing back a piece of Germany's rare Solnhofen limestone to show your students at the university. You might even add a fake price sticker to pass it off as a souvenir;

your story doesn't matter as long as it's short, sweet, and adds up. Chances are the security guards won't have the slightest idea what you're talking about and, reluctant to admit their ignorance, will offer a sage nod of the head as you are permitted to pass.

As you wing your way homeward, relish the fact that one of the most controversial and valuable linking fossils ever unearthed is now yours. The *Archaeopteryx* wasn't a dinosaur, it wasn't a bird; it was something in between. And so are you, in a way. A tunnel thief: not quite a mortal, but not quite a god either. Something different. Something evolved.

RODIN'S THINKER

LE PENSEVR
DE RODIN OFFERT

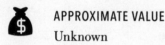 **APPROXIMATE VALUE**
Unknown

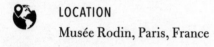 **LOCATION**
Musée Rodin, Paris, France

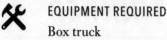 **EQUIPMENT REQUIRED**
Box truck
2,000-pound, 24-volt self-latching cargo hook
Electric winch with 5,000-pound pull
5,000-pound steel-braided longline
5-by-5-foot steel flatbed dolly with cast-iron casters
Technician's uniform
Tool belt
Insulated wire nut
Screwdriver
Steel bolt cutters
½-inch padlock with key
320-volt/100-volt step-up transformer
1-ton cargo van with aluminum loading ramp
   (5,000-pound capacity)
Inline control cable
Two-way radio transmitters (3)
Screwdriver
Insulated wire nut (10)
½-inch bolt cutters
High-energy diodes (4)
16-volt car batteries (20)

10-farad capacitors at 1,000-volt capacity (5)

AC rectifier

Jumper cables (10)

1,000 feet of ⅛-inch copper wire

10-inch-diameter iron core (50 feet)

1,000-volt cam switch

Nylon tension straps (10 to 20)

30 feet of pentaerythritol tetranitrate–rich detonating cord

Binoculars

ABOUT RODIN'S *THINKER*

Possibly one of the most daring campaigns in this book is stealing Auguste Rodin's *Thinker*, a statue so iconic that over twenty-eight copies, most of which were supervised by the artist himself, have been forged. *The Thinker*, originally named "The Poet," is said to be one of the most valuable sculptures ever created.

While there are many casts of Rodin's *Thinker*, ranging from seventy-three inches to over six feet tall, our focus will be a giant bronze cast, which weighs more than 1,900 pounds and sits in the entrance courtyard at the Musée Rodin in Paris. This statue was one supervised by Auguste Rodin himself; its worth is inestimable, but certainly ranges in the millions. One of the casts was recently sold to a New York collector for close to $15 million.

OVERVIEW

The sheer weight of *The Thinker* is going to be your biggest obstacle in this particular heist. It will require skill—specifically learning to fly a commercial helicopter—along with an equipment checklist that would give even the most seasoned thief pause. The plan involves a helicopter outfitted with a longline and precautions to ensure nobody can follow you. Furthermore, you will need a partner who will help loosen *The Thinker* from its concrete foundation so it can be easily hoisted into the air and carried to safety. The plan is bold, dangerous, and requires expert timing and guts of titanium alloy.

THE TEAM

The Thinker job requires a team of three: you and two other trustworthy individuals. For more details on how and where to find people willing to partner with you in a crime of this magnitude, see "Confidants and Profitable Partnerships" on page 21.

The Engineer (At a 40 Percent Take)

Your engineer must have an understanding of light explosives and be capable of handling high-stress situations. This person must also be physically strong: specifically, he must be able to carry his own weight for an extended period of time. A 40 percent split is recommended for this person due to the high risk of injury or death.

The Triggerman (At a 10 Percent Take)

The triggerman needs a basic understanding of electronics and must be someone you can trust behind the wheel of an industrial vehicle. A 10 percent split is recommended for this person, as her role is small and the risk of death, injury, or capture is minimal.

AN AERIAL VIEW OF PARIS

Paris from above provides a spectacular view. From the center circle of the Arc de Triomphe one can see the spokes of streets radiating out like a huge wheel; there's the beacon of light shining from the top of the iconic Eiffel Tower and myriad roundabouts encircling lush and sprawling parks. At night it all lights up like a Christmas tree.

Why is an aerial view relevant? Well, this job is going to require a helicopter—a big one. One that can jolt a 1,900-pound statue off its concrete foundation and support the dead weight as it sails away to freedom.

Héliport d'Issy les Moulineaux (LFPI) is a heliport just twenty minutes east of the Palace of Versailles. There are several companies based here that you can find online. They offer popular aerial tours of Paris and have a fleet of helicopters that rival some of the most sophisticated search-and-rescue units in the area. These helicopters are more than capable of hauling the statue's expected weight. With headquarters located just a few miles away, LFPI makes the perfect candidate. LFPI currently has around twenty helicopters, ranging from the Bell 206 JetRanger to the Hughes MD-500 series. Now is the time to hatch a plan for not only stealing one of LFPI's $150,000+ helicopters but for grounding the remaining fleet as well. To accomplish this, it's going to take time, capital, and months of preparation. Hey, no one ever said stealing Rodin's bronze masterpiece was going to be easy.

GROUNDING A FLEET OF HELICOPTERS

Grounding an entire fleet of helicopters is going to be by far the most risky element of the entire operation. You need to do this to ensure you won't be followed by anyone with eyes on the stolen helicopter's course, or escape will be futile. You're going to accomplish this grounding tactic by emitting a strong magnetic pulse, which will knock out LFPI's communications equipment completely.

In order to shut down air traffic at LFPI, you'll need a device that has the ability to knock out any electronics within a calculated range—it's called an electromagnetic pulse (EMP) device. An EMP device disrupts electronics using electromagnetic induction. This is how antennas, electric motors, transformers, and basically anything electronic operates.

Because you can't simply stroll into your local electronics store and pick an EMP device off the shelf, you're going to have to build one yourself.

BUILDING AN EMP FROM SCRATCH

The biggest problem with EMP devices is harnessing enough power to generate a sufficient burst of focused energy. It would take tens of kilojoules of energy to destroy circuits at the distance seen in a blockbuster film like 2001's *Ocean's Eleven*. But for your purposes, much less power is needed and can be obtained via a technique called *electric conduction*. This kind of electromagnetic burst should be enough to take down a nearby communications tower without causing complete and utter chaos.

> It's worth noting that protection from EMP is as simple as enclosing sensitive equipment in a metal box, called a faraday cage. Places like the Pentagon, NSA, and Fort Knox have aluminum mesh between the drywall to prevent an EPFCG (explosively pumped flux compression generator) from harming them. However, the walls of the air traffic control tower at LFPI are composed of concrete and drywall, so this shouldn't be a problem.

You have five capacitors that need to be wired together. This will be your means of storing the power that will later be dumped into the EMP transmitter. Chain your capacitors together using jumper cables, matching the positive and negative connections. With your capacitor chain finished, you will need to rectify the default alternating current (AC) power into direct current (DC). We'll do this by using a *bridge rectifier*.

A bridge rectifier is an arrangement of diodes that is used for converting an AC input into a DC output. Your diode bridge is assembled in the same way as your capacitor chain: They will be linked one after another to form a circuit. Use your remaining jumper cables to link up one end of your diode bridge to your capacitor chain. Now you have a safe way to transform your input polarity from AC to DC power.

A second circuit must be created that will be responsible for dumping the energy stored in your capacitor chain to a tightly wound copper coil. This is the actual EMP transmitter and is responsible for releasing and directing the electromagnetic pulse toward your target, which in our case is LFPI's primary air traffic control tower. To do this you're going to need roughly a hundred feet of ⅛-inch copper wire to be wound tightly around an iron core, which should be roughly ten inches in diameter and fifty inches in length. Start at one end of the rod and wind the copper tightly around your iron rod until you reach the opposite end. Both ends of the copper coil should connect back into the positive (+) and negative (−) of either end of your cam switch (this type of switch will provide you with a way to cut over to a high-capacity flow of electricity, safely and easily). It doesn't matter which end you choose, as long as the switch is toggled away from the coil itself. This will protect you from shorting out your EMP once you connect the power.

Last, you will need a power source and a transformer to step up the amperage. To do this you're going to create a third chain of twenty 16-volt car batteries. Link them together in the same way as before, leaving the last link on the chain unattached. The unattached end of your power chain will go directly to your 320-volt/1,000-volt step-up transformer, which will increase the voltage and speed up the charging process.

Once you have finished, you want to load the EMP into a box truck. This serves three purposes. First, you want to make the device, which will weigh over three hundred pounds, as easy to transport as possible. Second, the EMP must be sufficiently hidden from any wandering eyes. Third, and most important, you want to make sure the device is *not* grounded. A grounded device might cause your own body to complete the circuit, which could result in serious injury or death.

Part of your preheist planning includes learning how to fly a commercial helicopter; it's an investment of time and money vital to your success. You don't need a license per se, but you are going to need a solid understanding of the controls and, more important, the *feel* of flying a machine this big. It will cost somewhere between $2,500 and $5,000 to become properly trained.

Finally, you will need to educate yourself on longlines and how to fly with heavy loads in tow. This is fairly typical, as helicopters are often used to lift and transport heavy equipment. Specifically, you want to practice mounting and deploying a longline through the floor hatch while in flight. Depending on the type of helicopter you are in, this could be a manual process, meaning you might have to take your attention away from the controls temporarily to lower the line and cargo hook.

When purchasing your box truck you want to find an older model, circa the 1990s. Anything modern will most likely be computerized and will be susceptible to damage when your EMP is triggered.

BREAKING THE BREAKERS

For any of this to work we need to talk for a moment about breakers. A breaker box divides an electrical power feed into subsidiary circuits, while providing a protective fuse (or circuit breaker) for each circuit. Remember what happened the last time you tried to run your television, dishwasher, and vacuum at the same time? Your breaker box was the thing that protected you against a power surge that could have damaged your electronics or even harmed you, depending on the circumstances.

To get around this you're going to have to circumvent the air traffic control tower's breaker system several days before the heist, thereby removing protection from a surge. Here's how you're going to do it:

1. Your first order of business is becoming an electrician, which normally would require a four-year apprenticeship and journeyman license. However, for our purposes a uniform and tool belt should do just as well. It's amazing what you can gain access to with the right attire and a few well-placed accessories.

2. Once your disguise is in order your goal is to get to the air traffic control tower, located west of LFPI's Lot C, with *minimal* interactions. There are a couple different options here:

    a.   Walk in through the main gate, past the information desk, down a short hall leading out onto the flight deck, and head west directly toward the air traffic control tower. The key here is simply avoiding eye contact. If this plan fails try Option B at a later date, when the person who spotted you is not working.

    b.   Walk in through the main gate and find the information desk. Approach anyone there and ask if they can page "Larry Letchenson" (any fake name will do). When they can't find Larry, begin to get impatient by excessively checking your watch and rattling on about being late for your next job. When they ask what you are there for explain that you are checking the breaker system and that Larry said you would be on the list. As I've said before, this kind of thing is more an art than a science. People tend to avoid confrontation, so their natural reaction will be to let you proceed. In the event this does not work, simply leave. People typically forget faces in roughly three to six weeks. Try moving the calendar date and coming back later.

3. Once you arrive at the breaker box and are away from any suspicious eyes you can get to work. Don't worry; this is actually a lot easier than it sounds. Here's what you will need to do:

a. Find the breaker box on the backside of the air traffic control tower. It's a large gray rectangular unit secured with a padlock.

b. Remove the padlock with your ½-inch bolt cutters.

c. Open the cover and find the black plastic breaker switches.

d. Starting at the top, switch off the breakers one at a time.

e. After disabling each breaker, use your screwdriver to loosen the screw that secures the corresponding wire.

f. Bend the wire out of the way and cap it off with an insulated wire nut.

g. Repeat until there are no occupied breakers.

h. Close the cover and lock it with a new padlock.

Great, you're almost done. All you need to do now is clean up and get out of there. Remember to stay calm and collected. If you run into anyone just ramble on about having forgotten a tool and that you'll have to come back later. Remember, you always want your interactions with people to be at an absolute minimum.

THE SWITCH VEHICLE

A helicopter escape will be futile as air traffic is tightly monitored and you will have limited maneuverability due to the load you will be towing. For this reason you are going to use what is commonly referred to as a *switch car* to make your final escape. *The Thinker* is roughly the size and weight of a Smart Car, so you will need something relatively big, such as a one-ton cargo van, in which it can easily be loaded. Make sure you check the dimensions along with the axle weight of the truck to ensure it has the capacity to fit and haul the load.

When purchasing the truck do so in disguise. Use a fake ID, and pay with cash; you don't want to leave a paper trail. You can find what you're looking for at any one of the many used auto yards dotting the outskirts of Paris and Versailles. Remember, when making purchases like these, the smaller independent vendors are generally safer. Massive used car lots and auto franchises will most likely require extensive paperwork, which creates unnecessary risk.

Remember to use a disguise when shopping for vehicles. While it is estimated that over 65 percent of security cameras are fake, why take the chance of having your face captured on video? A good disguise is prudent in almost every circumstance. Always choose the safest path; this is a maxim that any thief should live by.

Once you have secured a transport vehicle you will need to install an electric winch with a rated line pull of five thousand pounds to hoist the statue into the hull. Also, if the van does not come with a loading ramp, you will need to install this as well. Last, make sure you have a five-by-five-foot steel flatbed dolly with cast-iron casters at your disposal.

Once you have secured the cargo van you need to find a landing site that will remain undisturbed for twenty-four to forty-eight hours. Here is a short list of criteria you should look for when seeking out a location for your landing and loading operation.

- Five to ten miles away from the Musée Rodin.
- Five to ten miles away from residential homes or businesses.
- At least a hundred feet from trees, power lines, towers, and other tall structures.
- A flat plot of land roughly two hundred feet in all directions.

While there are many places on the outskirts of Paris that fit this profile, I have already identified an ideal location near a golf course called Golf de Saint-Cloud, located at 48°51.304", 2°10.746". There you will have easy access to a discreet field where you can leave the cargo van unnoticed. Before you leave make sure the keys are somewhere in the van but hidden from sight and leave the van unlocked. Have your *triggerman* pick you up; the two of you will be back the following day via helicopter, to drop off the statue and load it into the van.

Everything should be coming along nicely now. At this point you should have your EMP ready for prime time, the breakers at LFPI should be disabled, and your truck should be ready and awaiting your arrival. Let's not forget your flying skills, which at this point should be second nature. All you need now is a way to get *The Thinker* off its concrete foundation and into the air.

SEPARATING *THE THINKER* FROM ITS BASE

Our main exploit for this operation is that bag checks, security cameras, alarm systems, and the like are all focused in and around the museum itself. The courtyard (albeit containing one of the most valuable pieces in the collection) remains largely ignored, simply due to the perceived impracticality of getting *The Thinker* off its foundation, out the front entrance, and into a vehicle. The point here is that no one will be anticipating burglary by airlift, which makes your job a lot easier.

However, before *The Thinker* goes anywhere we're going to have to figure out how to separate it from the stone foundation it's bolted to. The good news is that the sheer weight of the statue itself is what primarily fixes it to the base, along with eight modest anchor bolts. Beyond the bolts, the Musée Rodin has relied heavily (perhaps too heavily) on gravity as the primary means of keeping the statue restrained.

To bypass the steel bolts we're going to be using the magic of *detonating cord*. Detonating cord is a thin, flexible plastic tube filled with pentaerythritol tetranitrate, a sensitive compound that is easily detonated through a mechanical shock.

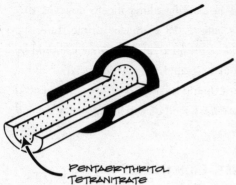

PENTAERYTHRITOL
TETRANITRATE

Detonating cord (also referred to as "det cord") will be used to shear through the bolts that lock the statue down, thereby freeing it from the foundational block.

It's worth noting that det cord is relatively safe to use due to the contiguous blast radius. This way your partner and his fellow museumgoers will be safe, as long as they are aren't crowding *The Thinker* when the detonation occurs. As an added safety measure you will be arriving promptly at 8:30 a.m., when the museum opens and while guests are still slowly trickling in.

> Before you can do anything you're going to need a method of triggering the det cord. This is remedied with an *inline control cable*, which can be found at a variety of online stores dedicated to construction supplies.

When the time comes, your partner should coil the det cord around the base of the statue several times over (see the illustration on the next page). This should provide enough redundancy

(TOP-DOWN VIEW)

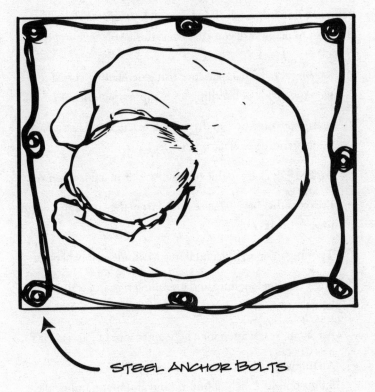

STEEL ANCHOR BOLTS

to amplify the blast and slice through the steel bolts. While all of this might seem a bit audacious to be doing during business hours and with guests and security roaming about, keep in mind that if properly timed the distraction of the approaching helicopter (piloted by none other than you) will keep people's eyes and attention exactly where you need them—up.

FINAL CHECKLIST

Before walking through the plan in detail, let's go through our checklist to make sure you have everything you need in place:

✓ An *engineer* with experience using detonating cord and who is capable of handling high-stress situations.

✓ A *triggerman* who can drive the box truck and has a basic understanding of electronics.

✓ An EMP device capable of 1,000+ volts of focused power.

✓ Breakers that have been removed from the air traffic control tower's breaker box.

✓ Training in operating and flying a commercial helicopter.

✓ High-tension longlines and grappling rigs and training in how to use them.

✓ An 8 a.m. reservation for a helicopter tour of Paris at LFPI.

✓ An unmarked 1-ton cargo van equipped with a 5,000-pound winch, 2,000-pound aluminum ramp, and flatbed dolly.

WALKING THROUGH THE PLAN

Assuming you are prepared, let's go through the plan for the day-of, step by step.

 7 a.m.—Triggerman

At 7:00 sharp your triggerman needs to be stationed at LFPI and ready to go. She needs to find a small service road north of LFPI, which will give her the contiguity and line of sight necessary for the EMP to be effective. The road is unnamed and does not exist on most maps (at least not as of publication). However, you can see this road in satellite images and should be able to find it easily en route. Take the road up a small hill; it will lead directly behind LFPI's main control tower, roughly fifty feet away. You should find sufficient cover behind a ridge that will completely hide the truck from sight.

The triggerman should park the box truck with the rear of the truck pointing in the direction of the control tower. The back hatch must be opened so that the EMP transmitter is pointing directly at the tower. This will ensure that the most concentrated waves will impact the radio transmitter, which ultimately is what allows helicopters to deploy. Not to worry, this method will not affect helicopters in flight so no one should be at risk. At the early hour you've scheduled, your tour will be the first to leave and therefore the full sum of the charter force should be grounded—except for you.

The triggerman should be disguised as a service

person in case someone wanders up the road. Use your two-way radios to communicate details to one another but remember always to use encrypted channels so your transmissions can't be sniffed out, whether on purpose or by accident. It will be up to you whether to call the mission a bust if someone becomes suspicious and you or your partner feels your cover is blown.

Be sure you never use names or other identifying information when communicating over public radio waves. Always use code names for people and places.

 7:30 a.m.—You

Arrive at the registration desk and check in for your tour—which you've already booked for 8 a.m. With small operations like LFPI, helicopters will typically take off one at a time. Yours should be the first scheduled departure. There will be a group of up to six tourists that will be boarding the helicopter with you. Don't worry about them; you will be flying solo when the time comes. Your job is to find a seat as close to the cockpit as possible and start familiarizing yourself with the control layout (with what you can see at least) so that when you are ready to fly, there is little delay.

Make sure to read the materials on the LFPI website so that you have everything you need, including a proper (fake) identification and a consistent disguise.

One key reason why LFPI has been selected (beyond its close proximity to the Musée Rodin) is its lax restrictions on allowed baggage. You will be exploiting this loose practice by bringing aboard a camera bag with two important pieces of equipment:

1. A two-way handheld radio.
2. A helicopter longline rated for 5,000 pounds of lift.

If all goes well your camera bag will go uninspected. If not, you still have a good chance of explaining the longline, which will be tightly coiled and might pass as some pro camera equipment. If not, the mission is a bust and you and your partners can walk away without any real harm done.

Your radio and any other electronics you want to keep intact should be stowed and wrapped in tinfoil. This will act as a Faraday cage that will protect your equipment from becoming damaged in the electromagnetic pulse that your triggerman is about to unleash.

7:45 a.m.—Triggerman

From her outpost, the triggerman can keep track of boarding tours with a decent pair of binoculars. Once she sees that you have boarded safely, she must begin charging the EMP by completing the circuit. Again, this means your cam switch should be toggled *away* from the EMP transmitter circuit and *toward* the circuit containing your battery chain, transformer, AC rectifier, and diode bridge. The device should begin charging immediately and will take roughly five minutes before it is ready.

Once the EMP device is sufficiently charged, the triggerman should throw the cam switch—but she shouldn't expect much. There will be no explosion or shock wave or loud bang. The pulse is harmless for humans and nearly undetectable. However, *you* will notice something is wrong, and that will be *your* cue to move to the next step.

8 a.m.—You

What you will most likely notice is a break in radio communication with the helicopter's transceiver. That will likely be followed by some panic and confusion between the pilot and other nearby LFPI staff. Once it is determined that radio communication has been compromised, you and the group will be asked to deplane the helicopter. You must appear cooperative, but you also want to take your time. Your goal is to be the last one off, which will put you closest to the aircraft.

This part may be a little tricky because what will happen next is highly unpredictable; you're going to have to improvise. At this point there should be total loss of radio communication with the primary control tower; there will be a level of chaos on the tarmac; staff will be distracted and panicking. This should be the perfect time to dash back to the helicopter, jump into the pilot's seat, take over the controls, and take off. This will most likely take longer than you would like. Getting familiar with the controls for any new vehicle takes a minute—but it shouldn't take much more than a few, or you could be in trouble.

You should now be airborne with no one knowing exactly where you are headed. By the time authorities have pinpointed your exact position, you will have had enough time to get to the Musée Rodin, pick up *The Thinker*, and tow it back to your switch car. Once you have made it to this point, your triggerman is effectively done. She can leave and continue back the same road she came in from. The odds that someone will figure out what happened before she has a chance to escape will be small. Trust could be an issue here—this is something for you to manage on your own. Your partner should go home and turn on the local news. Have her contact you if there is any evidence your whereabouts are known. After that, you should arrange a time at a later date where you can meet and make her whole.

Meanwhile, your engineer should be milling

around the outer courtyard of the Musée Rodin, acting as an art lover, and keeping *The Thinker* and the morning sky in sight at all times. Turn your radio on and signal to him that you are airborne. This is your partner's cue to make his way over to the target. With a cruising speed of 150 mph you should reach your destination within fifteen minutes.

The next twenty minutes of the heist are going to be the most dangerous. One wrong move here and you could wind up losing control of the helicopter and crashing into the courtyard of the Musée Rodin. Keep your cool and remember that you are nearly done. If all goes well you should have the priceless statue loaded into the cargo van and headed for safety within two hours.

Once you reach the Musée Rodin, position yourself directly above the statue and get eyes on your engineer. Once you've made visual contact begin your descent to fifty feet and maintain and lock in altitude, roll, pitch, and yaw. There are two reasons why this is a must: (1) It will be easier to position your longline and cargo hook directly above your target. (2) The helicopter's presence will be ominous and should send guests of the Musée Rodin scattering. This will ensure people's safety once the det cord is triggered (the blast radius is relatively minimal—no more than four to six feet, but better to be safe).

The engineer should wait until the last possible

moment before he begins to prepare the statue for lift-off. Because he has not yet entered the museum interior, his bags will have not been checked and therefore he need not worry about the spool being discovered. However, once this process has started, he will need to move swiftly. Once your helicopter is within sight, it is your partner's cue to begin winding the det cord around the base of the statue—four to six times, at least. For added assurance, he can wind the cord around the heads of each of the eight anchor bolts as well. Det cord has a strong punch at close proximity and should have no problem cutting through these bolts, especially when tightly coiled.

Coiling the det cord properly will take a minute or two, during which time you must keep the helicopter at a consistent altitude. The helicopter will be generating enough noise and wind to keep people's attention fixed on you, allowing your partner to finish.

Once the cord has detonated there will undoubtedly be panic. Use this to your advantage: Lower the grapple quickly. Throughout the rest of this process it's important that you and your partner are in tight communication with clear hand signals indicating to each other the following stages:

- Ground to pilot to stop the line descent.
- Ground to pilot to indicate the *grapple is secured.*
- Ground to pilot to begin lifting procedure.

Once the grapple is lowered, your engineer should thread it through the triangular-shaped hole between *The Thinker*'s thinking arm, leg, and chin. The following should happen in rapid succession:

1. The engineer secures the longline and signals.
2. Indicate you have received the signal.
3. The engineer latches on to the statue and signals.
4, Indicate you have received the signal.
5. Begin your ascent.

This next part is going to be the most dangerous (and possibly the craziest) thing you will have to do in any campaign in this book. *The Thinker* statue is very heavy. It weighs around 1,900 pounds, about the weight of a full-grown Kodiak grizzly bear. In addition, the bolts are not the only things holding the statue to the ground. The sculpture was installed on a concrete foundation and while the concrete was not designed to hold the statue in place, it is an additional seal that will require further upward force to break free from.

Not to worry. I have calculated that even the smallest helicopter in LFPI's fleet has the lifting force required to meet the combined demands of the weight of the statue, the engineer himself, and the force required to separate the statue from the foundation. However, be forewarned, the action of tugging and thrashing until the statue is separated from its base will be extremely perilous. Mishandled towlines are the number one reason helicopters crash. The added weight and sudden change in maneuverability require great skill. If you are not fluent in the operation of towing heavy things the chances of death or dismemberment are great.

Even though he has hooked himself onto the longline, the *engineer* will have to hang on tightly while taking care to protect his head; a sudden jolt could knock him against the bronze statue, rendering him unconscious. To avoid such a catastrophe he should make sure his arm is positioned between his head and the statue, providing sufficient padding in the case of a sudden shock.

You can break the statue away from the concrete base by pulling upward at a forty-five-degree angle. If the det cord was placed properly it shouldn't take much. Once you feel the sensation of a drop, straighten your pitch and ascend vertically with good thrust, thereby pulling the statue (and the engineer) directly off the base and into the air. As soon as you are certain of vertical clearance, head in the direction of your switch car; you have a partner and a priceless statue swinging on a cable twenty feet below you. Best not to think about it—remember to breathe and stay focused. This is a precar-

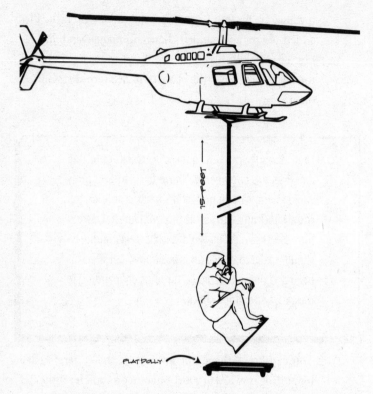

FLAT DOLLY

ious situation, and you can't afford to make any mistakes.

THE GETAWAY

Once you arrive, lower the statue (and your partner) carefully to the ground about ten feet from the back of the truck. Your partner's job is not over. He must dismount and remove the flatbed dolly. While he is doing this, pull the statue back *up* a few feet from the ground. Once your partner has positioned the dolly directly underneath the statue, follow his hand signals and slowly lower *The Thinker* directly down onto the flatbed.

Once it is in place, the engineer can unhinge the grapple and longline. Maneuver the helicopter out and away from both *The Thinker* and the switch car and find a safe place to land. Cut the engine and lights. Pause a moment to take a deep breath. While your adrenaline will likely be roaring, chances are no one will have any idea where you are. Remember, radio communication was disabled and your helicopter is not traceable when powered off. You have time to finish methodically.

Once you've calmed down a bit, make your way back to the truck and take the following steps:

1. Unreel the winch line in the cargo area of the switch car and attach the end around the thinking arm of the statue. This will enable you to hoist the statue onto and up the ramp.

2. Fire up the electric winch, keeping it in low gear. It should take fifteen to twenty minutes to pull the statue up the ramp and safely into the cargo area. Once it's in, secure the dolly to the cargo walls using nylon tension straps, thereby prohibiting it from rolling around during transport.

3. Lock up the cargo truck, have your partner jump in, and head out—any direction will do.

You and your partner will have to agree on a drop-off location. Have him take a bus or taxi home and assure him there is nothing to worry about: He *will* be made whole. If you have been upfront and straightforward with him so far, there will be no reason for him to doubt you. If he wants more information, such as a time line, simply explain, "This could take months, or even years. Once the transaction is complete I will contact you." Remain stoic. Plant your feet, stand tall, and demand his trust through posture and tone.

You are home free now—no one has any idea where you are or *who* you are. It's your choice what to do next, but most likely you aren't leaving Paris. Not with loot this cumbersome. Whether you can turn around this rare work of iconic sculpture in months or years is up to you. Just like *The Thinker*, you will have time to sit and ponder your next move.

KING TUTANKHAMUN'S GOLDEN DEATH MASK

APPROXIMATE VALUE
$1.5 million

LOCATION
Museum of Egyptian Antiquities, Cairo, Egypt

EQUIPMENT REQUIRED
Diamond-notch ¼-inch drill bit and 150-volt electric drill
Rubber mallet
Thick towel
Parachute cord (40 feet)
4-fluke steel grappling hook
Carabineers (2)
1-millimeter chain (3 feet)
Lock pick set (tension wrench, sawtooth rake, and short hook)
Bump key
Screwdriver
Latex gloves
Digital watch with backlight
Peanut or almond butter
Crackers
Bottled water (1 gallon)

ABOUT KING TUTANKHAMUN'S GOLDEN DEATH MASK

King Tutankhamun was an Egyptian pharaoh of the Eighteenth Dynasty, during the period of Egyptian history known as the

New Kingdom. The "Boy King," as he is commonly called, mysteriously died, leaving behind a glorious tomb filled with priceless riches. The tomb was discovered under a hidden step of an ancient Egyptian hut in 1922. It contained treasures that went undisturbed for over three thousand years, many of which were completely intact. The Egyptians buried their king with more than five thousand priceless objects, the most iconic and valuable being his jewel-laden golden death mask.

The mask is twenty-four pounds of solid gold, inlaid with carnelian, quartz, turquoise, obsidian, and other precious stones. The mask stands twenty-one inches high and contains two emblems on the forehead, the vulture and cobra; and on the shoulders, two falcon heads symbolizing Upper and Lower Egypt. The vulture (Nekhbet) and the cobra (Wadjet) protect the pharaoh in the afterlife and were considered sacred.

OVERVIEW

Sometimes the best thing you can do when trying to escape from a high-security museum, such as the Museum of Egyptian Antiquities (MEA), is to not leave at all. In this case, the authorities will believe you have gotten away, when in fact you will be hiding directly under their feet. With a police station only a few blocks away, attempting an escape *after* an alarm has been triggered would be nearly impossible.

The security applications in MEA use thermal imaging, motion tracking cameras in the halls and galleries, infrared fence beams surrounding each exhibit, and silent alarms placed at undisclosed locations throughout the museum. In other words, you're not getting in (or out for that matter) without broadcasting your presence to the Cairo police.

Getting in requires a critical skill I covered in Part I: how to cut through glass. One of MEA's most recognizable features is its famous glass ceiling, which was designed to bathe the gallery halls in natural light.

Getting out, however, will be much easier as you will be simply walking out the main entrance one to two days after the crime has taken place.

SECURITY AT THE MUSEUM OF EGYPTIAN ANTIQUITIES

The bloody revolution in 2011 in Tahrir Square has made Cairo one of the most dangerous cities in Egypt. The Museum of Egyptian Antiquities lies within walking distance of where protesters had set out to overthrow the regime of President Hosni Mubarak, causing the museum and other nearby institutions to tighten security dramatically.

Unfortunately, that didn't stop rioters from breaking into the museum in 2011 and destroying countless pieces of priceless artifacts. Although much was destroyed, King Tutankhamun's treasures were miraculously left untouched.

In light of these events, security at the Museum of Egyptian Antiquities is currently at an all-time high. During business hours security officials perform identification checks for every guest visiting the facility. The perimeter of the museum is heavily guarded during the day. The fire escapes, before 2011, provided easy access to the roof but they have since been secured—and in such a way that one can go easily down them, but not up. Expect to face a world-class security system and a police response time of no more than five minutes.

By the time you do leave you'll need a getaway vehicle at the ready so you don't have to go far on foot. Just like coming in, plan to trigger alarms on the way out as well. That's under five minutes to be in your car and out of the area completely.

THE GETAWAY VEHICLE

Your vehicle needs to be small and nondescript. Find something typical in color and body style—something easy to forget.

You also need a parking space close to the museum where you can stay parked *legally* for two to three days. Nile Corniche is a nearby outlet street just west of the museum and is dotted with public parking lots. Keep in mind: You need to be fit enough to make it by foot from the museum to the car, carrying a load of twenty-four pounds, in less than *five* minutes.

PREPARING FOR YOUR STAY

Five minutes may seem like a short time to be in the open, but with Cairo police breathing down your neck the statistical likelihood of getting away alive is small. And so you're going to extend your stay, thereby giving the heightened security time to die down.

To make your time as comfortable as possible you'll want to bring food, water, and something to keep you busy for a two- to three-day stay inside of the museum. I've included a few of the essentials in the list of needed equipment, like high-protein snacks and water, but feel free to include more, as long as you remember to keep the load of your pack *light*.

SCALING THE WALLS OF THE MUSEUM OF EGYPTIAN ANTIQUITIES

With the right tools, getting onto the roof of the largest and most secure museum in Egypt should be fairly straightforward. You're going to be making use of your grappling hook, some rope outfitted with footholds, and a three-foot chain to protect against fraying. There's more detail on this in Part I, "Utilizing a Grappling Hook to Scale Walls and Buildings."

CUTTING THROUGH INDUSTRIAL GRADE GLASS

The glass ceiling is not only the pièce de résistance of MEA; it's also its greatest weakness. You can get through this glass by using an electric drill with a ¼-inch diamond-impregnated bit. This will allow you to drill through the glass to create a perforated ring large enough to fit your torso through that can be dislodged with a forceful blow from your mallet. Again, we cover this in more detail in "Getting Through Glass," on page 14. It's going to be loud, but don't worry; the MEA cleaning crew is gone by 12 a.m. nightly.

DROPPING IN

Pull up your grappling hook and rope; you need it to climb down through the hole and into the museum. Secure your hook to something that will support your weight and throw the loose

end down into the museum. Use a thick towel to pad the sharp edges of the glass to protect against cuts or rope frays. You must descend quickly as you have probably triggered motion sensors by now. Stay calm and remember: You don't have to worry about an escape. At this point you are only minutes away from safety.

Once you are in, leave the hook and rope in place as a decoy. You won't be taking this path as your escape route, but you want the authorities to *think* you did.

NAVIGATING THE INTERIOR

The Museum of Egyptian Antiquities security system is made up of three primary components:

1. **Security cameras** to monitor every square inch of the museum's interior.
2. **Laser fences** surrounding each artifact.
3. **Thermal motion sensors** to detect movement.

When a motion sensor is triggered, a silent alarm will alert the local authorities, who most likely will respond immediately, given that they are close by. You can expect police to arrive within five minutes after the first alarm was triggered, which will most likely happen the second you drop down through the glass and into the museum. So move quickly. Follow the route illustrated on page 129; or use your flashlight and one of the museum directories—whichever is more convenient.

> While I typically recommend disguises whenever possible, the security cameras at MEA are *not* outfitted with infrared and therefore will not be able to capture detail unless there is sufficient light, which there won't be at this hour.

 For many years, rumors of a curse of the pharaohs persisted, emphasizing the early death of some of those who had entered King Tut's tomb. While new studies have shown this to be partly false, there have been many strange occurrences involving the people close to the excavation and handling of King Tutankhamun, including early death and dismemberment. I mention this only as a warning. While considering the details of the heist it would be prudent to keep in mind the artifact you are stealing was a deeply personal nod to an Egyptian king—one who was considered by some a god among men.

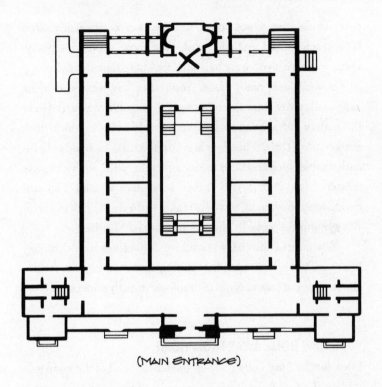

(MAIN ENTRANCE)

STEALING THE MASK

King Tutankhamun's Golden Death Mask is located on the main floor in Gallery A. You will find the mask sitting on a pedestal in the center of the gallery, encased in glass. Don't worry; the encasement is only aesthetic and can be shattered without any sophisticated tools. The museum keeps King Tut's Golden Death Mask under constant guard, but only during business hours, so you will be completely alone. Punch out a section of glass with a gloved hand or a mallet, making sure not to damage the mask in the process; it's delicate. Once you've knocked out a sufficiently sized hole, reach in and grab the mask—but move slowly, it's heavy. Once you have it you want to head back out to the main hall.

You're close, really close. You're heading west, down the main hall, away from the mummy exhibits. Once you arrive at the gallery entrance, look left, you should see a key-lock door marked *Staff Only*. This door is secured with your standard pin-and-tumbler lock and with the lock-picking skills you've already mastered (see Part I); this should be a piece of cake. You will need a tension wrench, sawtooth rake, and a short hook to get in. But a bump key wouldn't hurt to have on hand either.

Your heart is probably pounding. Authorities have definitely been notified and are most likely closing in. But not to worry; you're about to see just how easy it is to disappear directly under someone's nose.

YOUR NEW HOME AWAY FROM HOME

Look for the *Staff Only* door on the far east end of the main gallery on the first floor. This door will lead to a janitorial supply closet (blueprints are easier to obtain than you think). This room is important to you as it is positioned directly atop a *mechanical chase*. A mechanical chase is a hollow section of floor (or wall) that operates as a ductwork for conduits, wiring, and other building infrastructure. The point here is that it is large enough to hide in, totally undetected, and for days at a time.

Once you've picked the lock, make certain you've gathered up everything behind you. That means gear, shoe marks, blood, sweat—everything. Unscrew the access panel and shimmy down into the chase cavity. Both you and the mask should fit through easily enough.

You will find the space to be comfortable, with enough head-room to sit upright, but not stand. You won't be able to screw the floor panel back in place from inside, but do your best to see that it is properly seated in position so as to not arouse suspicion.

> You might be thinking we've left something out by leaving the door unlocked, and we have. There is no way to lock the door behind you without risking time, of which you will have very little. Don't overestimate the authorities. They will be focusing on other things: the exits, the rope, the shattered glass–the rooftop. A detail like this will be minor and will most likely be overlooked.

At this point it will be clear that the collection's most cherished artifact has gone missing. The museum will be flooded with authorities. They will find a shattered rooftop window, a hanging rope, and grappling hook; enough for them to make the assumption that you are either on the roof or already gone.

Here is where one of the most important characteristics of a good thief comes into play: patience. You should have enough food and water to last you roughly forty-eight hours, about the amount of time it will take for things to settle down in Cairo.

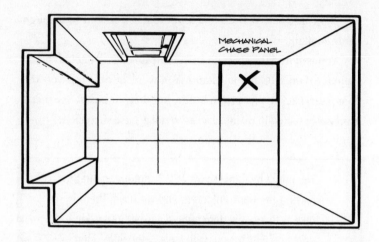

Forty-eight hours may seem like a long time, but don't get brazen and try to connect to the museum's WiFi network. That's a surefire way to blow your cover. A book and a flashlight can keep you company while you wait it out. In fact, this will be the perfect time to flip through this book in search of your next scheme.

THE GETAWAY

Your escape will not be dissimilar to your entry—you're playing the clock here, attempting to exit the museum before the police have a chance to arrive. Here's how we'll do it.

The Museum of Egyptian Antiquities relies on state-of-the-art security systems that are nearly impossible to disable. This means that the minute you crack open the supply closet door you can expect the silent alarm to trigger and alert the Ministry of Interior. You will have only a handful of minutes from the time you leave your hideout to navigate to the west exit, find your vehicle, load in the loot, and escape. You can expect the reaction time to be even quicker this time around, as the authorities have not yet found you and will be on high alert regarding any security issues related to the MEA.

The best time for your escape is at least forty-eight hours after the hit, and between 12 a.m. and 3 a.m., when cleaning crews are off duty. Your car should be parked legally and close by, as covered earlier. Leave your belongings behind; you don't have time for that. If you don't have a criminal record and you plan to retire after this, fingerprints don't even matter. Of course you've been cautious by wearing latex gloves, but let's be honest: No one has biological archives these days unless you're CIA. Don't overthink it.

Hug the mask to your body and run like you've never run before—police and canine units are likely minutes behind you. Your rental car should be only a few minutes away, under a fake name of course and paid for in cash (as covered in Part I).

Once you and the payload are safely in your car, you're basically home free. Your goal is to get as far away from the museum as possible without being noticed. It will take about an hour before roadblocks are put up; by then you will either be back in your rented room or on your way to Cairo International Airport to catch a redeye.

As you drive safely within the speed limits, observing all traffic lights and stop signs, courteously allowing pedestrians the right of way, you may want to reflect on the rich life of King Tutankhamun before he was sealed away in his adorned sarcophagus. Countless servants to fulfill his every whim, the best chefs to prepare every meal, the most beautiful women available at the crook of a finger, massaged and pampered—with all he had, how strange that he died so young. Of course, with money and power come enemies. But then again, doesn't everything?

THE CROWN OF QUEEN ELIZABETH

APPROXIMATE VALUE
$12 billion

LOCATION
Jewel House, Tower of London, London, England

EQUIPMENT REQUIRED
Picsima soft tissue printer
3D LifeViz II portable scanner
Phone repairman uniform (hard hat, utility belt, boots,
    etc.)
Lineman's handsets (2)
Alligator clips, small (4)
Stripper/cutter pliers
Binoculars
Lock pick set
British Suit
PAX makeup kit
Spirit gum
X-Acto knife
Wig
Unmarked van

ABOUT THE CROWN OF QUEEN ELIZABETH

The Crown of Queen Elizabeth is one of the most valuable
pieces in Britain's renowned collection known as the Crown
Jewels. The crown is part of the regalia and vestments worn by a

British monarch when a sovereign is being crowned. The crown is made of platinum and is encrusted with precious stones, including what is possibly the most famous diamond ever discovered by man—the Kohinoor, also known as the "Mountain of Light."

While the Kohinoor diamond has never changed hands through a documented sale, it is estimated to be worth roughly $10,000,000,000 (almost as much as the crown alone). Although the crown is encrusted with other jewels, it is the 106 carat Kohinoor diamond that is the real treasure here. With a valuation in the billions, it makes the Crown of Queen Elizabeth the most lucrative job in this book. However, you will need to be cunning and bold in order to pull this off. And most of all, you will need the best disguise ever conceived in the history of high-stakes thievery.

OVERVIEW

In designing this heist it became apparent, early on, that the weakness you need to exploit is not within the security systems, but in the rituals and traditions of the Yeomen Warders, also known as the Beefeaters. This exploit aims at the chink in the armor of the Royal Guard, which is simply *reliance on people over systems*.

While the details of the Jewel House security system are mostly unknown, what *is* known is that there are special circumstances when the crown is left exposed and vulnerable, outside the walls of the London Tower and beyond the protection of the Beefeaters. One of these special circumstances is an annoyance that even a queen can't avoid: jewelry repair. For this important task, the queen must rely on the one and only Crown Jeweler.

Let's start first with how the position of the Crown Jeweler came to be and who that person is today.

THE CROWN JEWELERS

In 1843, Queen Victoria appointed famed London jeweler Garrard & Co. to the position of Crown Jeweler. Garrard & Co. earned this role based on their extensive experience cutting and handling some of the world's most precious stones. In 1852, they were assigned the perilous task of cutting the raw Kohinoor stone into a faceted diamond. The risk was enormous. Cutting a brilliant diamond this large had never been attempted in known history, and the possibility that the stone would crack during the process was considerable. Garrard & Co.'s Kohinoor diamond is considered to this day to be one of the most beautifully cut large diamonds in the world.

However, in 2007, in a shocking and mysterious move, Buckingham Palace announced that their 164-year relationship with Garrard & Co. would be coming to an end and that G. Collins & Sons (another local luxury jeweler) would be appointed to the position of Crown Jeweler. Some think this is due to the expert craftsmanship of Harry Collins, which attracted the queen's attention in 2000 when she looked elsewhere to create something special for her mother's hundredth birthday. The result was a centenary rose brooch, a carved and hand-painted reverse intaglio in rock crystal, which Her Majesty has since inherited and wears in public frequently. In this case it was a rose that stole the queen's heart away; quickly thereafter the role of Crown Jeweler was given to Harry Collins himself.

So why is Harry Collins so important to this job? Simple. Outside of the Royal Family, the crown jeweler is the only person who is allowed to physically handle Queen Elizabeth's crown. In a monarchy steeped in history, ceremony, and ritual, the oversight we will use to gain access to the crown is the new and unacquainted addition to the Royal Family: G. Collins & Sons—better yet, Harry Collins himself.

Just one year ago, prosthetics and makeup would have been the best technique to alter your face to resemble Harry Collins's. While makeup will still play an essential role now in defining skin pigment and tone, a starch-based "ink" will be the material used to create a soft, flesh-like mold, uniquely designed to fit *your* face. And the technology needed to achieve this? A 3D printer designed by Fripp Design and Research that can print silicon indistinguishable from human skin.

3D PRINTING A FACE

Fripp Design and Research are the creators of the first 3D printer, named Picsima, which is capable of outputting a unique material required for soft tissue prostheses. This material has the same soft qualities of human skin, while capturing nuances as slight as pores and wrinkles. This emergent technology was developed by companies that design and manufacture prosthetics for faces. The molds can be tinted and made to blend in perfectly with the skin areas to seamlessly replace missing facial features, like noses, ears, and chins.

While not developed and designed for your purposes, this printer can output silicon features that can be applied to create a hyperrealistic replication of a person's face, undetectable even when close up. The printer can be purchased on Fripp Design and Research's website. You need to fill out the application that states for what purposes the machine will be used (and you have to pay them $10,000). There is no process of validation so feel free to put anything in the application, as long as it sounds legit. You can tell them you are an educator looking to use the printer for medical research or a soft prostheses startup that is testing 3D models. The process is simple and, in less than six weeks, you should have the printer and a sufficient supply of silicon ink to manufacture everything you need to transform yourself into a completely different person.

Now that you have the means to print realistic prosthetic skin, we'll have to come up with a method to customize the cast to fit your face seamlessly, while making sure the outside resembles Harry Collins in every detail.

TWO FACIAL CASTS

To do this right we're going to need *two* separate casts—one of your face and one of Harry Collins's. *Your* cast will be used to create the negative—the inside of the prosthetic—while Harry's face will need to be molded, from the ground up, by a professional artist. The end result will be a digital model of both faces that you can upload directly to your 3D printer.

Let's start with Harry: We're going to have to create his face from scratch, and the likeness must be impeccable, so we're going to need the help of a talented special-effects artist. The best place to find the person we need is the film capital of the world: Hollywood, California.

Hollywood is home to the bulk of the film and television industry, so finding a top-notch special-effects artist is like shooting fish in a barrel. The *Hollywood Reporter* is an online publication in which local special-effects artists can publish classified ads. You will find everything from photographers and sound engineers, to actors and makeup artists. While studios typically produce work solely for film and television, it's not uncommon for artists to take on smaller jobs for individuals and independent projects.

Contact the special-effects studio by phone, not in person. Your story is simple: You are looking for a lifelike bust of a friend for an art installation you are working on. If questioned for details simply reply, "The project is very hush-hush so I'm not at liberty to say."

This type of realistic sculpt can take up to six weeks to complete and will cost $3,000 to $5,000, depending on the studio's reputation and experience. Make sure you look at other work they've done (even the smaller special-effects shops have websites) to ensure that their quality is up to your standards.

You will need to provide the artist with source material, which is essentially a collection of photographs and videos of Harry Collins that your artist can work from. Finding these images online won't be difficult; Harry Collins has been in the limelight enough wherein his face has been sufficiently covered by UK news stations. However, while Collins has appeared on television from time to time, he is not prominent enough to be recognized by most British people, let alone by Hollywood types.

> If you're wondering why you aren't hiring the studio to create the finished prosthesis itself, the answer is simple. Your true face can never be seen by anyone. You must retain your anonymity and this demands that you take on some of the work yourself.

Once the finished work is complete, have it delivered to you via post. Now you will have a plaster analog of Harry Collins's face. What you need next are two digital scans—one of you and one of Collins. To generate the 3D models you're going to use a handheld 3D scanner called a LifeViz II—it will set you back around $25,000 but is completely necessary as we're going for the highest fidelity possible. When you are done you will have two detailed 3D digital models: one of your face and the other of the face of Harry Collins. You are going to use these two files to create a third file, which will be a composite of both. The backside of the cast will be a negative mold of your face that will fit you perfectly. The front will be that of Harry Collins.

Follow the instructions provided with your 3D printer software to create the composite, using the two digital files. This is the basis of the Fripp Design and Research technology and should be outlined in detail in their documentation.

APPLYING THE PROSTHETIC MASK

Everything is now in place to create the soft tissue prosthetic that will be used to transform your face to that of the queen's personal Crown Jeweler. Your new face will be printed, layer-by-layer, in spongy flesh-like silicon. Using an X-Acto knife, remove the openings for your eyes, mouth, and nostrils. For best results, cut along the natural creases in your face or where the silicon is thinnest. Once you have a clean prosthetic with seamless edges, it's time to apply it. When the time comes you will need to perform these steps on the fly, so experiment with this process until you get comfortable with it before proceeding.

You can use spirit gum (available at any online makeup store) to apply the prosthetic to your face. First, apply a thin coat evenly to the inside of the prosthetic. Then, gently press the prosthetic to your face, starting with the nose and moving outward to the edges. This will help avoid trapping air bubbles under the silicon.

You should begin to see the likeness of Harry Collins emerging already. Now for the fun part: applying the skin tone and nuances that make your new face come to life.

HAIR, MAKEUP, AND WARDROBE

Depending on the length of your hair you may or may not require a wig. Below is an example of Harry Collins's hairstyle. As you can see, it is two to three inches long, wavy, but not curly, slightly thin on top, brown with some gray on the sides, and combed back behind the ears. If you can't cut and dye your hair to match Collins's, try checking out wig shops until you find something that matches.

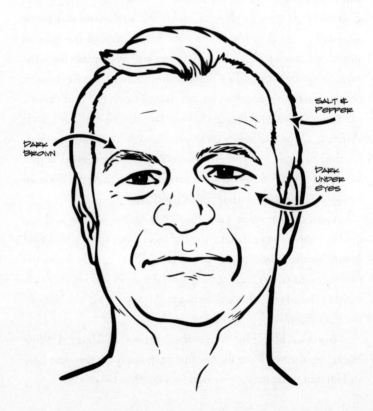

This next step is where the likeness of Collins should really start to come together. Purchase a PAX paint kit online that comes in a variety of skin tones. You want to start with a good foundation you can build on—it's all about experimentation, so have fun! Overdoing makeup tends to look obvious, so start with one color and work from there. Again, this is not something you will perfect on your first attempt. It will take time to find the shades and techniques that work best for you.

In addition to hair and makeup, don't forget about Collins's attire. We've seen many times throughout this book how power-ful simply *dressing the part* can be. Collins is a well-groomed gentleman and a Cornwall-born scholar. He dresses in suits when conducting his business: typically British traditional, double Windsor tie, black or brown buffed shoes, and tweed

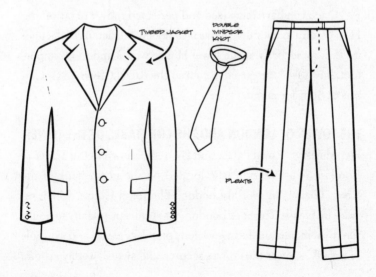

jacket with elbow patches. You will find exactly what you're looking for on Savile Row in London's Mayfair, and you should spend at least $500—else expect to raise eyebrows.

SPEAKING THE PART

Dress is important, but so is your voice. Harry Collins speaks in a soft south Cornish accent, which you must learn—although you will be saying very little. YouTube is a great resource where you can find tips and techniques to help you mimic dialect in a variety of regions. Study these videos and learn the nuances of the south Cornish accent. Don't worry so much about precision; you won't need to trick anyone who is especially familiar with Collins's voice, as will be explained later. What is necessary, however, is that you can carry on a conversation with people from neighboring regions without arousing suspicion.

Once you have rehearsed and perfected the art of becoming Harry Collins, your next move is to review the details of the plan itself: how security at the Jewel House works and more important, how to get the queen to courier the Royal Crown to G. Collins & Sons for maintenance.

THE TOWER OF LONDON AND THE CONSTABLE OF THE TOWER

Her Majesty's Royal Palace and Fortress, known as the Tower of London, is a historic castle located on the north bank of the River Thames in central London. The Jewel House, which resides inside the Tower of London, was built specifically to house the royal regalia, including various priceless jewels and symbols of royalty, such as the crown, scepter, and sword. Today visitors can tour Her Majesty's regalia, which is on display for the public but still used by the queen for coronations and other royal events.

The Constable of the Tower is the most senior appointment at the Tower of London, where the Crown Jewels are kept. The current constable is a celebrated and decorated British Army officer, General Lord Dannatt, resident Governor of the Tower of London and Keeper of the Jewel House. Lord Dannatt is one of the queen's closest allies. He is well respected among the British Royal Guard, the Yeomen Warders, and the most powerful members of British Parliament.

> Lord Dannatt has met Harry Collins on only a few occasions. This offers some leeway with your accent, which may not be as polished as you would like. The most important thing here is not that you sound just like Collins but that that you maintain an accent that Englanders, like Lord Dannatt, will believe.

FIT FOR A QUEEN

Weighing in at just over four pounds, the queen's crown is a mite heavy for the wearer; to prevent it from falling off during a coronation or some other public event, a good fit is a must. While the crown is seldom worn, it is the Crown Jeweler's job to ensure the queen's regalia are kept up and ready to be worn publicly at a moment's notice, should some unforeseen event occur.

In the past, when maintenance was needed, the *king's* crown was delivered directly to the private practice at G. Collins & Sons in Tunbridge Wells, UK, and worked on in secret, despite the modest security at G. Collins & Sons. This is our aim for the queen's crown, with the reasonable assumption that all of the queen's regalia follow the same maintenance pattern.

On a day of your choosing, G. Collins & Sons is going to make a call to Buckingham Palace and ask to be transferred to General Lord Dannatt, Constable of the Tower. Harry Collins will be making the call personally to inform the crown holders of a potentially faulty clasp that puts the crown in danger of becoming loose during wear. But it won't be Harry Collins making the call; it will be you.

HIJACKING A LANDLINE

In order to pull off this job you're going to need to have a basic understanding of landlines and how to exploit them. Similar to phone tapping, which allows you to listen in on phone calls, landline hacking allows you to make calls on behalf of the hijacked phone number. This is relatively easy to do.

The first thing you will need is a proper disguise. You will be posing as a telephone repairman—so an orange jumpsuit, hard hat, utility belt, and boots will do the trick. Once you have everything in place you want to make your way over to 78 High Street, Royal Tunbridge Wells. It is best to do this during a weekday, sometime between 8 a.m. and 11 a.m., so as to maximize your chances of getting the Constable of the Tower on the phone.

You need to find a lineman's handset (also called a *butt set*), which is a tool used by repairmen to test phone lines for activity. Butt sets are basically trussed up landline phones with a small dialing pad and two alligator clips, for tapping directly into a line. You can find them online for under $100. Of course, make sure you cover your tracks by using an encrypted web browser, as covered in Part I.

The utility box for G. Collins & Sons is located in the back of the building on the wall that faces the alleyway. You might have to use a little force to get inside but don't worry; to the passerby you are just a repairman doing your job. Inside the utility box you'll find a pair of green and red wires devoted to each line. The green wire is your positively charged current, and the red handles negative current. All you need to do is connect the alligator clips to the correct color-coded wires and you're done.

With unfettered access to the line, it's time to test your handiwork by making a call. Try a local number; if the tones are accepted and your call goes through, then you're in business. Now anyone you call using your butt set will see "G. Collins & Sons" on their caller ID.

Dial +44 (0)20 3166 6000, which will get you to an operator at the Tower of London. It's up to you to work your way through the departments until you get a hold of Lord Dannatt himself. Now keep in mind, this might seem strange to an operator. Why would you, the Crown Jeweler, be calling a *tourist* line to reach someone whom you have direct access to? The best strategy here is to simply be incredibly friendly; apologize for calling this main line, and say you've misplaced Lord Dannatt's contact information. Your name (which should be familiar among Tower of London staff), the caller ID (which will corroborate your assumed identity), and your friendly demeanor should be enough to get you transferred up the chain of command.

If you aren't able to get Lord Dannatt on the phone, offer to call back. Leaving a message won't be possible because you will have no way of intercepting the returned call. It might take several attempts to connect to the right people and ultimately get the boss on the line.

Once you are on the phone with General Lord Dannatt your goal is to keep the conversation short and to the point. In your learned south Cornish tongue, introduce yourself as Mr. Harry Collins. Keep in mind, Collins is a removed member of the royal staff and has most likely had little direct interaction with Lord Dannatt. Get the accent right, as discussed earlier, and he should be none the wiser.

It might be a good idea to put some notes down on paper that you can use to rehearse and better prepare you for the big day. Here are the points you want to touch on:

1. There is a fastener called a *low-loop* that secures the Kohinoor diamond to the crowns velvet inlay. The fastener has been fail-

ing on similar jewelry and therefore should be replaced. Stress that the Kohinoor is at risk of falling off completely if it is not repaired soon. Your goal here is to create a false sense of urgency.

2. While you are open to doing this at the convenience of the palace, request that the day fall on a Saturday or Sunday, so you can work undisturbed. Weekdays simply won't work for our purposes (as I'll explain later) so you need to get a commitment for an upcoming *weekend*.

3. As the modifications needed are relatively straightforward, the crown will be available and ready to be picked up the following day. This should make the decision easier for Dannatt to make, as the crown will be back on display within twenty-four hours.

If all goes according to plan, Lord Dannatt should set an appointment with you to bring in the crown and have the fastener replaced. You should have several weeks to prepare because a transport will have to be arranged by the Queen's Guards, which is tradition when moving any of the items in the Crown Jewels collection from one place to another.

If something goes wrong—such as Dannatt becoming suspicious or not being available at all—then you have lost little. You are merely a voice on one end of a phone that will be traced back to someone else entirely. It's your call as to if and when you want to try again. However, if you are successful, the last leg of this heist should be as simple as sitting back and waiting to receive a billion-dollar package.

To get you inside of G. Collins & Sons, where the Queen's Guard will be expecting to deliver the Royal Crown to Harry Collins in person, you'll have to conduct a classic jewelry store bust.

BREAKING INTO A JEWELRY STORE

Weekends at G. Collins & Sons are quiet. There is no staff, no cleaning crew, and most important, no security personnel. It is during this period that interception of the crown will take place. But first, you're going to have to find a way in to the store itself, which is going to take some work.

> You'll want a van, or some other unmarked vehicle, parked within walking distance–no more than a block away. During the weekend parking is readily available so you shouldn't have a problem.

The break-in should occur the day of your scheduled appointment with Lord Dannatt and his guards, either a Saturday or Sunday. Once again, you will be going incognito as a phone repairman, but will change into Harry Collins once you're inside, so make sure your duffel bag contains your prosthetics, makeup, suit, shoes, and anything else that you've prepared for your transition.

While G. Collins & Sons handles some of the most precious jewelry in the world, it still remains a small-town jeweler with ordinary customers, like you and me. This is not to say its security isn't state of the art—it most definitely is—and so in this final stretch, it is imperative that you become familiar with the specifics of the security systems, and their weaknesses, at G. Collins & Sons Jewelers.

THE THREE PILLARS OF SECURITY AT G. COLLINS & SONS

The security you're dealing with won't come close to anything we've seen in previous chapters. Our entry, this time around, is going to involve bypassing a set of simple systems that even a beginner should be capable of cracking. Let's look at what we're dealing with before jumping into the exploits:

1. There are heavy-duty door locks and deadbolts on all three doors, two in the front and one in the back.
2. All windows are outfitted with aluminum conductive security foil and high-grade glass break detection.
3. There are a total of six security cameras capable of high-resolution video and thermal sensors with complete coverage of the showrooms.

There are typically two phases of detection in these types of security systems. The first, an *intruder* phase, signals guards, key holders, owners—basically anyone other than the police. The *confirmation* phase, which occurs upon a second detection, immediately alerts authorities. If you activate the confirmation phase, expect armed personnel to arrive within five to ten minutes.

But you're going to need a lot more than ten minutes to pull this off: You're going to need eight to ten *hours*. You'll also need lights; you will have to appear as an open business, for the purpose of meeting Lord Dannatt. This is not a smash and grab job! There will be no smashing *or* grabbing. Therefore, the security system must be deactivated completely.

THE ALARM SYSTEM

The alarm systems in most jewelry stores of this size use phone lines to transmit silent signals to stakeholders and police. This means an alarm system can easily be disabled if you know how many lines are going into the building and how to bypass cut-line detection. In your case, exactly two lines come into G. Collins & Sons, and they both come in from underground on the southeast corner, providing service to both floors of the building.

Most systems like these have a feature called *cut-line detection*. This feature does exactly what it says: It detects if the phone line has been cut, or more accurately, when a signal cannot be detected for some arbitrary duration of time (usually around thirty seconds).

Your lineman's handset is going to prove useful once again. This time, however, you will require a second handset because there are *two* separate lines that need to be dealt with. Once both lines are cut your handsets will act as a receiving signal to trick the phone company into *thinking* the connection was only momentarily down. Here's how to do it:

1. There is a gray box near the electric meter on the backside of Collins & Sons where the main line comes in from the street. The box has two sides, one of which is accessible only to the phone company and is locked with a padlock. You can easily remove that with a pair of twenty-four-inch bolt cutters. Do it.

2. Once the box is opened you will find a network interface device, which is where the lines from the street and the lines going into the building are connected. Using your stripper/cutter pliers, cut the red and green wires for either one of the lines (it doesn't matter which you start with) and strip the ends. *Once you do this you will have roughly sixty seconds to complete the remaining steps.*

3. Using the alligator clips, connect one of your butt sets to the exposed line, making sure to pay attention to the colors.

4. Turn on the handset and set it to *manual disconnect* mode. You want the signal to remain on and open until the battery dies. This should give you roughly twenty-four hours of solid signal, which is much more than you'll need.

5. Repeat steps 1 through 4 for the second line and you're good to go.

Find a place out of the way to hide the handsets from view. Lord Dannatt and the Royal Guard will most likely enter through the back, where deliveries are normally made, and the last thing you need is for someone to get suspicious. Once you're done, get out of there. You want to monitor the location from afar with a pair of binoculars on the off chance something didn't work and police have been dispatched. If twenty minutes pass and there is no activity, you can assume it's safe to return.

Go around back again and find a small window; there are two (see the map below). While the glass-break detection will begin transmitting the intruder signal (along with the motion sensors), no one will receive it. However, you want to avoid the sound of breaking glass as to not attract unwanted attention. For more information on how to silently penetrate glass, please refer to "Getting Through Glass" on page 14.

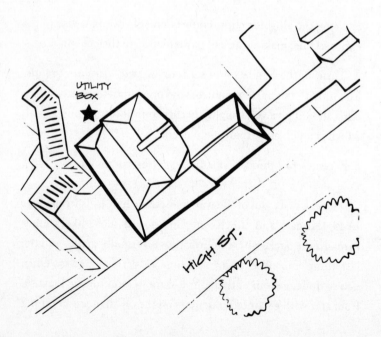

SETTING UP SHOP

From the back of the building and facing the street, you will see a door to your right that leads down a short hallway and to a private workshop, on the left. This is Harry's office and it may be locked. If so, you should be able to pick it easily (lock picking was covered in Part I).

Once inside Harry's office you can relax and begin the process of getting into character. To make your interaction with the Beefeaters believable you must be comfortable with your environment. This is *your* office, where *you* make beautiful and priceless pieces of jewelry. While Queen Elizabeth's crown is arguably one of the most valuable treasures in this book (and possibly the world) it was Harry Collins himself who hand-crafted the re-creation of Henry VIII's Imperial Crown in the very room where you are standing. You see, the Royal House is built on *personal* relationships, so while these surroundings may seem ill-equipped to receive an item of such value and prestige, in the eyes of the queen this workshop is a trusted place. Remember, the person you are masquerading as is highly respected and treated like royalty.

Keep all of this in mind as you apply your makeup, don your wig, and slip into your suit. This is a good time to study your script as well. Transforming into Harry Collins is both a physical and mental exercise and by the end you should feel confident enough to face anyone.

THE DELIVERY OF QUEEN ELIZABETH'S CROWN

Before I jump into the handoff itself, it is important that I review the possibility of some British vernacular popping up in conversation that could put the entire operation at risk if responded to in a way that arouses suspicion. For this reason we're going to add an additional ruse to mask your true identity: a head cold. This little trick will help you keep from cornering yourself with an errant comment; it's as easy as faking a slight cough and speaking through a handkerchief to muffle your voice. This additional subterfuge will also help to expedite the handoff and minimize opportunity for error, on your part.

> If you're not familiar with phrases such as dog's dinner, spanner in the works, arse over tit, bits 'n bobs, her majesty's pleasure—or any other colorful British slang—it would be wise to react with coughing when presented with something confusing.

There it is, a knock on the back door. The Constable of the Towers (or one of his men) has arrived to deliver your $12 billion package. Of course, exactly who delivers the crown and how it will be delivered cannot be precisely known. However, you can assume several of the Queen's Guards will be present. All that *can* be done to prepare you for what might be behind that door when it opens *has* been done. It's up to *you* now.

Leverage your newfound confidence as Crown Jeweler and everything should be fine.

> It would be disingenuous to say the odds of deceiving one of the most respected and decorated men in British Parliament are great being that success will be entirely in *your* hands. A small slip up at this point will undoubtedly lead to a swift arrest by the British Army, likely stationed directly outside the door.

Here are some important things to remember when greeting your guest(s):

- Keep at least three to four feet of distance between you and anyone else at all times to avoid someone noticing a prosthetic seam or errant makeup. (The fact that you have a head cold will make this less suspicious.)
- Stay friendly and calm.
- Keep your responses to a minimum; speak only when it is required that you speak and use your cold as a veil whenever possible.
- When referring to the queen always use the words *Her Majesty*.
- End your sentences with *sir* whenever possible. In other words, keep it extremely formal, *sir*.

Beyond that your goal is the same as Lord Dannatt's: a safe and swift transference of the queen's crown. Your job at this juncture is simply not to get in the way. Exactly how this will play out cannot be foretold. It may require some improvisation or even manipulation. Make Lord Dannatt comfortable leaving the crown in your possession. Given your extensive background with precious jewels and your personal relationship with the queen, this should absolutely be achievable.

Stay friendly (simple pleasantness will take you a long way in this business) and let Dannatt excuse *himself* so you can begin your craftsmanship in privacy. If you feel the meetup is dragging on, you might need to chauffeur things along with a simple line, "It will be a pleasure, as always, to aid in the conservation of such a fine piece of craftsmanship." And with that, end with a reassuring smile.

THE GETAWAY

Use your best judgment as to how long to wait before you leave. Keep in mind, there should be no need to rush out. When you do leave, you're going to do so as the phone repairman, not Harry Collins (the last thing you need is for Mr. Collins to be recognized on the street; that would not bode well for you). Place the queen's Crown in your duffel bag (heavier than you expected, isn't it?) along with the clothes and mask of Harry Collins. Exit the building and walk casually to your van, which should be parked nearby.

As you drive off, obeying all the traffic rules, let the feeling of victory wash over you. You now have in your possession one of the most valuable and iconic pieces in all of the queen's regalia—the Crown of Queen Elizabeth II! Encrusted in its platinum coronet (along with other priceless jewels) is a diamond considered by many to be the world's most valuable—the Kohinoor diamond, the "Mountain of Light": at 106 carats, its value is said to be in the *billions*.

Pity though it may be to dismantle this historic tiara, it will most likely reap you the greatest financial rewards to do so. But first, do place it on your *own* crown, gaze into a mirror, and picture the king's life you will soon be living.

THE CODEX LEICESTER
by
LEONARDO DA VINCI

FRIDAY 12 DECEMBER 1993

APPROXIMATE VALUE
$30 million

POTENTIAL LOCATIONS
The Solomon R. Guggenheim Museum,
New York City
The National Gallery of Art, Washington, DC
The Art Institute of Chicago
The J. Paul Getty Museum, Los Angeles
The de Young Museum, San Francisco
The Museum of Fine Arts, Houston

EQUIPMENT REQUIRED
Mercedes-Benz S550, 4Matic AMG
Large enclosed transport vehicle
Midsize SUV
Jaws of Life (5,000 psi) and eDRAULIC cutters
Martin Professional Atomic-3000-DMX strobe system
with radio trigger (3)
525 millimeter by 60 millimeter refractor computerized
telescope
Light-weight welding goggles (3)
Long-range, two-way radios (3)
8 copper wire mesh, 0.028-inch diameter (10 by 10 feet)
Laptop computer
Reflective safety vest
Yellow hard hat

ABOUT THE CODEX LEICESTER

Purchased in 1994 by Microsoft founder Bill Gates, the Codex Leicester remains one of the most valuable books ever written. Historians believe this thought-provoking journal written by Leonardo da Vinci to be his most insightful and inventive work. While the value of the codex may not rival that of his most famous creation, the *Mona Lisa*, the Codex Leicester contains in it ideas, inventions, and observations that have continued to confound experts to this day.

The manuscript does not take the form of a single linear script, but is rather a mix of Leonardo's observations and theories on astronomy, the properties of water, rocks, fossils, air, and celestial light. In its meager seventy-two pages, the Codex Leicester predicts plate tectonics and theorizes on the movement of water; it expounds insights on moon luminescence and explanations of why oceanic fossils can be found atop mountains.

Surprisingly there is still controversy regarding the translation of the content, despite how well the pages have been preserved. The problem is that most of the text was written in Leonardo da Vinci's characteristic mirror writing—that is, it was written backward. While the reason for this is largely unclear, it is thought that da Vinci was attempting to hide his scientific ideas from the powerful Roman Catholic Church, whose teachings sometimes disagreed with what Leonardo observed.

OVERVIEW

When Bill Gates purchased the Codex Leicester, he selflessly decided *not* to keep the original manuscript hidden away from the public. Instead he had each page digitally scanned at the highest possible resolution and made the pages available to anyone with an Internet connection. In addition, Gates decided that it would also be unfair to choose a single home for such a magnificent work; and so once a year the Codex is put on public display in a different museum around the world.

While this presents a logistical challenge, it also presents an opportunity to intercept the Codex during transport from one museum to the next. While museum security from city to city is nearly impossible to anticipate, the process of moving the piece is consistent from year to year and therefore can be predicted and exploited. To do so, we'll look at the storage, transportation, and security measures taken to move the Codex Leicester to its next destination each year.

THE TEAM

The Codex Leicester job requires a team of three, and each one of you needs to be comfortable with performing highly precise and choreographed behind-the-wheel maneuvers and in the presence of other drivers. In addition, the two team drivers need to be able to stand up to the law and stay quiet should they be taken into custody (a very real possibility in this case).

HOW TRANSPORTATION OF THE CODEX LEICESTER WORKS

Each museum's respective staff transports the Codex Leicester while overseen by the Gates-appointed historian and curator, Fred Schroeder, who is responsible for the organization and management of the codex's yearly trip from museum to museum.

Throughout its travels, this delicate journal is protected in a sealed glass case called a *Climabox*. This protective case helps keep the work secure while at the same time maintaining a climate-controlled environment for its fragile pages. The case is made of polarized glass, which protects the document against light that can be potentially damaging.

There are several stages the codex will go through before it can reach its final destination. Here they are, in order, from the removal of the codex from the departure site, to its installation at the destination site:

1. The Codex Leicester is unmounted and then sealed in a scratch-resistant case called a Climabox.

2. The Climabox is wrapped in palette tape, then bubble wrap, and finally placed into a container or a crate. The art is held in place using Styroboard mounts and any excess space is packed tightly with alfalfa hay.

3. Before the crate is sealed, a small battery-powered GPS device and RFID chip are mounted to the inside of the crate. This allows the art to be tracked and identified if it is lost or stolen.

4. The crate is then transported (under supervision) to the museum's loading bay, where armed security supervise it until transportation arrives.

5. The codex is transported in one of the most advanced armored cars ever conceived, either directly to the destination museum or to a nearby airport.

6. The art handler, the museum staff, and the private security company predetermine the ground route. Because of the difficulty they present to thieves trying to make a quick getaway, the team normally chooses a highly trafficked route. The private transportation company provides the armored transport vehicle and driver; they also include a motorcade consisting of one to three unmarked security vehicles with highly trained and heavily armed drivers.

7. Once the codex arrives at its location, the art handler (the only person with keys in his possession) unlocks the truck. The codex is then carefully removed by transport team and moved by hand to another loading bay.

As you can see, there is concentrated security at every step of the transportation process, so we need to find a way to get a hold on the codex without putting you (or your partners) in danger. To do this you're going to need to get your hands on an armored car of your own.

Since a private firm handles the transportation of the Codex Leicester, it is helpful to have a general understanding of the type of insurance carried on invaluable artifacts. Transportation companies that deal in priceless goods are heavily insured to protect against damage or theft. Thus, in the case of a disaster, the art owner will be paid handsomely. This kind of premium protection opens up holes in the transportation process. For instance, no one is going to risk his life against a potential threat. (And that is not to say there will be any threat.) However, when a transport crew perceives a possible threat, they are trained to transition to a lock-down phase, which involves halting transport and doing whatever necessary to preserve the safety of the crew. The financial risk of someone becoming injured or worse is far greater than the loss of a piece of art.

This is important to underscore, as the fleet of vehicles and uniform (and armed) personnel can prove to be intimidating. Keep in mind, you most likely won't find vigilantes in an operation like this, which is privately owned and grossly over-insured. Armored truck officers have the second highest death rate in security and so safety is the first priority when shipping cargo like this. Protection against theft itself is a distant second.

FINDING A DECOY CAR

For this campaign you will be using the bulk of your budget to purchase a replica of the armored car that has been used to transport the Codex Leicester within the United States in recent years: the Mercedes-Benz S550, 4Matic AMG, high-gloss machinery gray. This is the car the Gates team has historically used to transport the codex in coordination with the sending or receiving museum. The S550 has been retrofitted with bulletproof glass, a ballistic steel cage encasing the cab and trunk area, armoring around the fuel tank and battery, and a plastic lining inside each tire to protect against flats or blowouts.

However, beyond the tinted windows, the armored version of the S550 *looks* identical to the consumer version, which is going to make things a lot easier for you. This is going to be a "for sale by owner" transaction, to avoid the paper trail that goes along with buying from a dealership. You need to find a 2012 model, and it must be customized with blackout tinting on all windows, except for the windshield. (If you don't get the correct year you run the risk of someone noticing even a slight change in the body type.) Once you have the model, color, year, and appropriate tinting, the cars will look nearly identical.

Here's the thing: Since we are swapping *your* S550 for the *armored* S550, we need a way to hide the resemblance of the two vehicles *before* the switch takes place. Two identical cars driving in proximity only raises eyebrows and puts the entire operation at risk.

PARAMAGNETIC PAINT

Paramagnetic paint is truly a sight to see. Imagine being able to hit a button and change your car, instantly, to any color you want. The technology exists today and works by running electrical current through a special polymer applied to the body of the car. This special polymer contains particles of paramagnetic iron oxide. With the applied electric current, the position of the oxide's crystals is adjusted, affecting their level of light reflection and thus changing the color of the vehicle on the fly. Amazing, right?

Since the aim is make the color change as dramatic as possible, it is recommended that you choose something light and bright. Yellow, green, red, or orange will all provide sufficient contrast to the S550's machinery gray.

While this technology is fairly new, most high-end body shops will be able to apply the polymer and wire up a toggle switch that the driver can access from the console. You're going to need to find someone you can trust to do this work. Whether it's someone you already know, someone whom you've paid off, or someone whom you've cut into the action—your goal is to find someone that you are confident will keep quiet, regardless of who comes sniffing around after the fact.

This gets even more complicated. So far you've got the decoy vehicle and a way to change its appearance with the flip of a switch. But now we need to find a way to get the armored S550 (and the driver) off the street and out of view entirely.

FINDING A TRANSPORT VEHICLE

You're looking for an enclosed transport vehicle for a single midsize sedan to hide the S550 inside of. This enclosed trailer can be any depth, so long as it fits the length of the S550; however, the width of the trailer must be no more than seven feet wide. If you can't find something with the proper width, you will need to modify the interior so there is no more than seven feet from wall to wall.

Next, you need to rig the trailer gate to a motor drive that you can access from the truck cab's interior. This will allow you to open, close, and lock the trailer completely from inside the cab—all while driving.

Finally you will need to outfit the trailer interior with tire ramps (see the illustration below). This will allow for the car to roll up and over the blocks, thereby trapping the vehicle (and the driver!) inside, even if the car is thrown in reverse after the fact. I'll elaborate on this further momentarily.

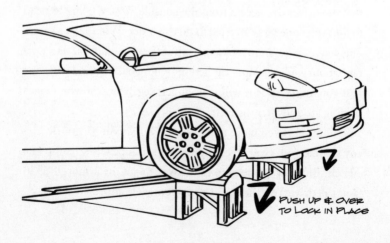

PUSH UP & OVER
TO LOCK IN PLACE

The last modification you will need to make is simple, but is going to take time. You need to transform the trailer into a giant Faraday cage. A Faraday cage is a metallic enclosure that prevents electromagnetic fields from entering or escaping it (as covered earlier in the Rodin's *Thinker* campaign). Don't forget, we have GPS and RFID devices *inside* the trunk of the car, which will give away your position to anyone looking for a signal. The ideal Faraday cage consists of a seamless, perfectly conducting *shell*. Using a fine-mesh, copper screen to line the interior allows you to construct a shell that shields all signals emitting from the Climabox that houses the Codex Leicester. You are looking for a specific type of copper mesh called 8 copper wire mesh, 0.028-inch diameter, which can be purchased in bulk on a variety of websites that sell raw materials. Again, remember to make this purchase on a *secured* Internet connection. We've covered this in detail in Part I.

> While the trailer itself is most likely aluminum, which will do a good job of blocking most radio waves, the Faraday cage is a good idea to make sure no signals can get in or out of the trailer.

Great, but how are you going to get the armored S550 trapped inside your enclosed transport trailer? Well, we'll do this with a little help from a third vehicle.

THE "SHOVE CAR"

The last vehicle you're going to need is a *shove car*. The shove car will do just that: It will shove the armored S550 up the ramp (don't forget, the ramp has already been lowered) and into your enclosed transport trailer, where it will become trapped and closed off by simply flipping a switch from inside the cab.

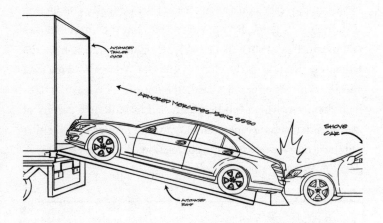

A large and powerful SUV should be enough to do the trick. However, it should be outfitted with a grill (to protect the engine) and it must be easy to maneuver, yet still have enough power and traction to shove another car forward a full car's length. If timed right, the receiving truck should be *braking* simultaneously, thereby sandwiching the S550 and forcing it easily up and into the trailer (see the illustration above).

Finally, once you have the driver, the armored transport vehicle, and the codex tucked away in your possession—you will need a safe place to go.

THE HIDEOUT

Immediately after the vehicle switch, you'll need a hideout in which the entire cab and trailer housing the S550 will fit. A mid- to large-size garage will do just fine and should be easy enough to rent. Find a place nearby, with easy access, and run by people who don't ask questions or who can be paid off in cash. For now all you will need to have ready are your Jaws of Life, which you will be using later to extract the codex from the trunk of the S550.

Once the shove car driver has completed the job (ramming the S550 up and into the trailer), he or she needs to make haste to the garage and await your instructions.

PREDICTING THE TRANSPORT ROUTE OF AN ARMORED VEHICLE

As in any heist, stealing the Codex Leicester involves a degree of ambiguity. However, this campaign in particular requires improvisation above and beyond what one might expect, due largely to the fact that the exact location of the codex cannot be known. Thankfully, figuring this out should be feasible with some guesswork and a little luck.

You will know the codex's departing site and finding the destination site should be as simple as making a few phone calls. The codex's next destination will be made public a few months

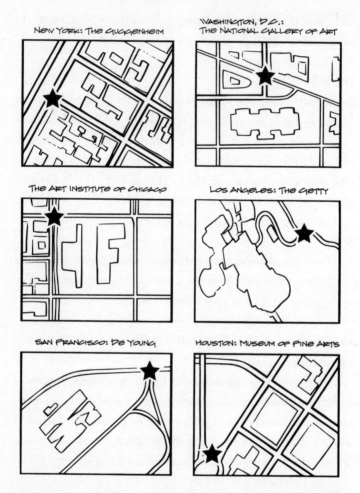

before the end of its stay each year. You want to make sure the codex is departing from one of the following museums: the Guggenheim in New York City; the National Gallery of Art in Washington, DC; the Art Institute of Chicago; the Getty in Los

Angeles; the de Young in San Francisco; or the Museum of Fine Arts in Houston. These museums all have *two* key things in common: They each meet the criteria for housing the Codex Leicester, and they are all located in areas that use common routes for the transport of high value objects.

> See the maps on page 176 for the routes typically used by each of the museums listed in the text. As you will see, each map has been labeled with a star, marking the inception point where the actual heist will take place.

HOW TO HIDE A LUXURY CAR IN PLAIN SIGHT

To execute a proper bait and switch, you not only need to mimic the target vehicle but must also hide the armored S550 from view altogether. So far, you have a color-changing car that can transform itself into a perfect replica of the S550, which will mislead the motorcade at the flip of a switch. But how exactly do you hide a car being shoved by another car from behind and into a massive transport trailer?

You'll employ a distraction technique commonly used by magicians: *misdirection*. Misdirection is an occurrence that takes attention away from the action—in this case the action of swapping two vehicles in plain sight. For our purposes only a moment is needed—a *flash* if you will.

A FLASH OF LIGHT

To generate a flash strong enough to temporarily mask the vehicle switch, take a tip from photography. To control lighting in an outdoor environment it is sometimes necessary for a photographer to overpower the sun's light by using strobe lights. Most strobe lights are within the 200 to 400 watts per second range, but temporarily blinding an intersection full of drivers will require something with a little more punch.

You are after the Martin Professional Atomic-3000-DMX, which produces a whopping 3,000 watts per second of blinding luminescence. You'll trigger three of these strobe bays using a radio-powered trigger that comes with each unit, allowing you enough time to swap the vehicles directly under the noses of a vigilant motorcade (and anyone else within eyeshot, for the matter).

The result of a strobe this powerful is a burst of bright white light so intense that it momentarily activates the photoreceptor cells in the eye, temporarily blinding anyone (without sufficient eye protection) for approximately five seconds. It is during these five seconds that you will turn your decoy vehicle into the target of the motorcade as well as hide the original S550 from sight completely.

Remember: You will need to purchase three pairs of welding goggles, one for each member of your team. The truck and trailer, the decoy car, and the shove car must each contain a pair of goggles to protect the drivers against the strobe flash.

You have nearly everything you need in place, but for all of this to work your timing must be perfect. That is, you need to know exactly when the armored S550 will be departing so that you and your team can be ready and on the road. This type of information cannot be attained by simply calling the museum; you will only raise suspicion. For this you will need eyes on the departing museum's loading bay 24/7.

24/7 MONITORING

The next thing you will need to do is set up some tech to monitor activity at the museum's loading bay. To keep this simple and private, find a high-rise hotel room within a few miles of the museum with a line of sight to the loading bay. Hotels are easy enough to book with fake identification and in some cases won't even require a credit card (when cash is paid up front). This should not be a problem as all of the museums listed are located in urban areas and are all encircled by tall city buildings.

You'll need a computerized 525 by 60-millimeter refractor telescope, which you should be able to find online for around $3,000. This telescope will provide enough magnification to identify what is moving in and out of the museum.

In addition, you will need a way to capture the telescope's signal and transmit it through an Internet connection. This can be done by linking the telescope to a laptop (via USB or WiFi connection) and connecting remotely to the computer from a different location via a secure proxy. Just follow the instructions that came with the telescope and you should be ready with eyes on the loading bay 24/7.

INSTALLING THE FLASH BAYS

You can learn the approximate date of transport by keeping track of when the Codex Leicester exhibit closes. Museums typically don't hold on to works that aren't being publicly exhibited for long periods of time. You should plan on the transport of the codex taking place five to ten days after the exhibit closes.

On the day the exhibit closes, act swiftly. First, install the strobe bays at the location indicated in the map on page 176. Configuring the bays should be relatively straightforward, and again, should be covered in the product manual. Use a standard reflective vest and yellow hard hat when installing the strobe bays to avoid suspicion.

You want to place them in locations that are not easily accessible to prying eyes. The strobe bays are small and durable enough that you shouldn't have to worry about leaving them for several weeks on end, as long as they are relatively hidden. See the illustration on page 176 for the precise positioning of the strobes.

THE PLAN AND EXECUTION

You and your two drivers need to be stationed within five to ten minutes of the museum for the remainder of the job. Everyone must be on call and ready to leave at a moment's notice. Organize a sleep schedule to ensure 24/7 monitoring of the museum's loading bay. Museums have been known to do these things in the early morning hours, so don't be surprised if activity fires up at 3 a.m. It can happen any time, so you and your team must be ready the second it goes down. You are looking for a rectangular crate being loaded into the trunk of a machinery gray Mercedes-Benz S550 4Matic AMG. This is unique to the codex, which will make the possibility of a false start highly unlikely.

The person on shift who catches the loading of the codex taking place must alert the rest of the team immediately. *You* are driving the truck and trailer while your partners (it doesn't matter who) man the decoy vehicle and shove car. You will need to be in constant communication via three two-way, dual-band radios at all times. Once the transport is green-lit the following phases must be carried out with precision:

Phase I: When the call is made, it is everyone's job to get to his respective vehicle and begin loosely patrolling the streets surrounding the museum. At this point all radios are on and lines open. Keep in constant communication with your team: You need to know where they are and when or if anything out of place occurs. It may take time for the motorcade to organize itself, but with three cars circling, one of you is bound to catch the departure as it occurs. When this happens you want to move into Phase II: getting into position.

Phase II: This requires that the trailer be positioned in the same lane as the S550. It should start two to three cars ahead. You're going to leverage the ubiquitous annoyance we all feel when driving behind someone you can't see around. In other words, those cars behind you will change lanes, especially if encouraged with some excessive brake tapping. At the end of this phase you, the truck and trailer, should be positioned *directly in front* of the armored S550.

Phase III: Your decoy car should be set to a bright color; green, red, or yellow will do. Once it is, get the decoy S550 positioned as close to its counterpart as possible, but *not* behind it. The point is that you must be in a position and angle that will allow you to take the place of the S550 within seconds. Don't worry so much about the motorcade. You probably have something presidential and robust in mind, but this is a simple art transport and is a fairly modest operation. You won't be seeing cruisers lined up back to front; it's going to be much looser and fluid than that. In other words: You shouldn't have a problem getting close—or even *beside*—the armored S550.

Phase IV: Finally, the shove car should be ready to move in directly behind the S550. It's best if you position yourself this way, but as long as you are able to get behind the car once the signal occurs, you should be fine.

You need to practice all of this (on random cars of course) in the days beforehand to get a feel for how each phase plays out and how long everything will take. Pick a car to test with and see how quickly you can get your team in position, in front, to the side, and behind it. If it's taking more than ten seconds, keep practicing.

Now that everyone is in position things are going to start moving fast, *very* fast. To best prepare you, I've enumerated each step below. These steps should be burned into your brains, because everything must happen within a five-second flash of the strobe, else the mission will be a bust.

Once the motorcade is within five hundred feet of your strobe bays, ready the strobe trigger and inform your team to put on their protective goggles. The flash must be triggered when the armored car is within a hundred yards of the trigger point or else you won't have sufficient time.

Once the strobe bay is fired the following steps must take place in rapid succession:

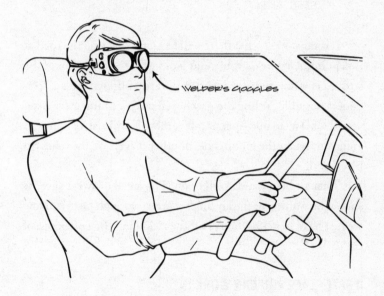

WELDER'S GOGGLES

1. **You:** Open the trailer gate, lower and extend the ramp.
2. **Decoy car:** Toggle the decoy car's color to match the S550's machinery gray.
3. **You:** Hit the brakes on the truck and trailer. If all goes

well the real S550 will have no time to lock up the brakes and should roll right up the ramp and into the trailer.

4. **Shove car:** Should be ready to assist in ramming the S550 from behind, should the momentum of the braking alone not be enough.

5. **You:** Trigger the trailer gate to close and lock the S550 inside.

It is most likely that there will be some chaos on the road at this point. Anyone en route and looking in the direction of the strobes is going to have been temporarily blinded, so an accident is possible. While the prechosen trigger points have been vetted for low- to mid-speed traffic, there is still risk of injury to you, your team, the motorcade, or other drivers on the road. So be careful!

That all being said: Well done. The smell of sweet success should be wafting in the air. But we aren't through just yet. Now we just have to get both cars off the road (and the codex out of the car).

A SAFE PLACE YOU CAN WORK IN

You need to get the trailer en route to the garage and off the road as quickly as possible. Remember, things are going to be messy, so take advantage of the confusion by getting the trailer out of sight before someone becomes suspicious. Have your friend in the shove car meet you there; he should take a different route.

The GPS signal from the S550 has gone dark at this point,

which has most likely alerted the motorcade that something is wrong (if the confusion on the road hasn't already). You're banking on the fact that, as far as everyone is concerned, the S550 is safe and still moving along its expected route. This is not to say a Code Red will not be issued. It only underscores that if everything has gone to plan the attention will be fully on the decoy car, and with the real S550's GPS signal trapped in the Faraday cage, you need not worry about someone detecting its location.

Get the shove vehicle off the road and out of sight as quickly as possible. Your driver should head to the garage and wait for your arrival.

As far as your decoy driver is concerned, he needs to keep pace and stay aware of the fleet of panicked police and security vehicles trailing behind him. The goal here is simple: Your driver needs to keep the police distracted just long enough for you to make it safely to the garage. Since all radio communication has been mysteriously cut off, it will be expected that he continue to the destination, rather than pulling over and making himself vulnerable to attack. Keep in mind, when moving payload this valuable the worst thing you can do is stop. The goal of the motorcade, in case of emergency, is to keep the payload traveling to safety. So no turning, no pulling over, no change in speed, nothing.

You, on the other hand, need to act fast. If the guy in your trailer is smart he will be laying on the horn by now, considering the dead radio and the fact that he is literally trapped inside his vehicle (which is to say, trapped inside your trailer). Get to the garage quickly, pull inside, and close up shop. You've got work to do.

> At this point it can be argued in a court of law that you are holding a captive prisoner. This is not far from the truth and so it's important to note here that at this stage there is no going back. The screams of a man held captive would shake any decent person to the core; but you have a $30 million prize coming to you–along with every single on-duty police officer in the general vicinity. It's time to stay focused.

Once inside the garage, you are ready to open the trailer hatch and begin prying at the trunk using the Jaws of Life. Yes, your shove car driver should be there, in the garage, waiting to help you. Armor or no armor, the Jaws of Life should be able to tear away at the trunk, layer by layer. If you've picked your location well, you should have enough privacy to work on the trunk for as long as you need. No one knows the car is missing and when they do, they still will have no idea where it is. Just keep in mind where the driver is: locked in a cage, essentially.

Meanwhile, your decoy driver should keep the motorcade moving as far away from you as possible. Once a safe distance is reached (three to five miles should do), he should simply pull over and park. It's difficult to predict what might happen next;

how long it will take security to approach the decoy vehicle, for instance. However, the driver has done absolutely *nothing* illegal and has *no* ties to you or the operation. He must maintain his innocence when questioned, and he should be prepared for things to get tense. An arrest, while completely unsubstantiated and highly illegal, *may* occur. Your driver needs to anticipate this with the full understanding that the police have no right to hold him longer than forty-eight hours without probable cause.

Back at the garage you should be closing in on the Codex Leicester. Once you get the trunk open, take the crate that is carrying the codex and move it to the shove car. Then open the garage and leave with your partner, coolly and calmly.

> Leave one of the roller doors to the shop open so the GPS signal can be discovered and the driver of the S550 can be freed quickly.

THE GETAWAY

Drive. It doesn't matter where, but you want to be far away from this place. Drop your partner off somewhere and assure him you will make contact. This is definitely one of those windows down, music up moments in your life. Breathe it in.

Leonardo da Vinci once wrote:

It had long since come to my attention that people of accomplishment rarely sat back and let things happen to them. They went out and happened to things.

Gone are the days when you sat back waiting for your future to come upon you. Your future is *now*. It sits in the trunk of an ordinary car, heading down an ordinary road—one of the most famous and intriguing journals in the history of humankind. The mind of a painter, a sculptor, an architect, an inventor—scribbled out in backward handwriting and illustrated with careful craft—Leonardo da Vinci's priceless manuscript. The jewel of a plan executed with a precision that would have inspired Leonardo himself. Congratulations on a job well done.

PART III
THE AFTERMATH

Selling Goods on the Black Market

THE PROFITABLE HEIST

Let's be honest—the ultimate goal after pulling off any heist is *profit*. By studying factors such as value of the target, operational expense, time line, risk of capture, and buyer availability, you can begin to focus on which campaigns have the best margin for success for *you*, therefore yielding the most lucrative return on investment. However, identifying the campaign that makes the most sense for you is only half of the picture. An art thief is just a collector if she can't find a buyer willing and able to put up the cash for an illicit transaction.

Once you have successfully completed any of the campaigns in this book, you will begin what is known in the underworld of stolen collectibles as the *silent period*. You have in your possession a priceless piece of history, but all your hard work is meaningless without an exit strategy. The untimely or indiscreet sale of a stolen collectable has been the ruin of many a thief. There-fore, your objective now is to keep quiet and stay out of the pub-lic eye. This period can last months to years, depending on the notoriety of the artifact and the media coverage of the crime. Once the heat dies down you will be ready to begin considering potential buyers. This can take months to years, and you will know when is the right time by keeping tabs on the investigation, simply by watching the news.

FINDING A BUYER

Finding someone with the means and appetite for crime is an art in itself. Target investors, entrepreneurs, art collectors, and art dealers—these are the people that you want to become close with. However, finding accomplices *capable* of committing a crime of this magnitude is its own challenge. When vetting buy-ers there are three simple questions you should ask yourself—and if the answer to any is unclear, simply move on.

1. Do they have sufficient familiarity of the piece and an appreciation for its significance and value?
2. Do they have the financial means necessary to exe-cute a six- to seven-figure all-cash transaction?
3. Do they possess the ethical makeup necessary to follow through with a deal of this magnitude in to-tal privacy, without threat of betrayal?

An easy way to start is to locate people with criminal re-cords for crimes such as infringement, fraud, extortion, embezzlement, and theft—you get the idea. Whichever direction you choose, keep your focus on ferreting out the psyche of buyers and dealers (both of which are potential candidates) with the thirst and acumen to go the distance. Learn about your customers. Do the research. Surround yourself with the superrich by working your way into the upper echelons of society. Attend art openings, benefits, auctions, black-tie affairs, and political fund raisers—wherever you can find the power players of your city. Right now your goal is to become a familiar face and to identify people that meet the benchmark, all without drawing attention or suspicion to yourself.

OFFLOADING YOUR LOOT

Here's the bottom line: Art thieves inevitably must sell—or "fence"—the works they steal to shady dealers at significantly reduced costs; unless they plan on hanging on to the piece for sentimental value. The dealer who buys the stolen piece will then pass it off to another collector in a private sale. The collector either keeps it or sells the work again, thereby obfuscating the transaction chain through simple arbitrage. In the United States, for instance, buyers can be prosecuted under the National Stolen Property Act only if the government can *prove* that they knew the item was stolen to begin with. Once a painting (or some other artifact) changes hands two or three times, buyers can plausibly (and sometimes honestly) claim that they thought it was legitimate.

There's another way to offload your loot, but it involves working with the lowest of the low: insurance companies. We've touched on insurance for assets—such as art, antiques, jewelry, sculpture, fossils, and other priceless collectables—when outlining the Codex Leicester campaign. What we haven't covered is how susceptible insurance companies are to *art ransom*. Claims like these can be in the billions, so insurance companies have a checkered history of working closely with criminals and keeping the feds out of the picture completely.

Here's a scenario Hollywood *does* get right: An anonymous phone call, a 2 a.m. meet-up at an undisclosed location, and a briefcase filled with nonsequential, unmarked bills—this is truly how these meet-ups go down. You will need a facade that evokes danger, even when there is no danger whatsoever: A modulated voice over the phone, slow echoing footsteps in a cavernous parking garage, dark sunglasses, and a smoldering cigarette; these are all devices used to keep a situation from going off the rails completely. They are designed to instill fear in others and to keep people from taking advantage of you.

The process is relatively simple: Find the insurer responsible for the piece you have stolen; relationships between museums and insurers are no secret; all you need is to ask around. Once you have a name it's as simple as making an anonymous call from a throwaway mobile (we call these *burners*) to explain that you have the item with you, that it is safe, and that you are ready to negotiate. The collection fee is yours to decide; we've provided the appraised value; you decide the markdown. It's as simple as that. Unless of course, they've called your bluff—in which case you might end up at the bottom of a very deep body of water.

Money Laundering

HOW MONEY LAUNDERING WORKS

Having sold your goods on the black market, you're probably sitting on a pile of cash so big you've had to count it by *weighing* it. Best to get it all into a bank account quickly, right? Not so fast. Before doing anything with your abrupt infusion of cash you must ensure the *government* knows how much you have and where it came from. Sounds ridiculous? Well, so does a new Bugatti parked in the driveway of a schoolteacher, or a carpenter, an insurance salesman—or whatever it is you *actually* do for a living. To make your money legit you're going to have to come up with a story that explains where it came from, and just like everything in this book, your planning and your story need to be airtight. Far too many criminals slip up in the final stretch, losing their millions and winding up in high-security lockup.

The process is called *money laundering*, which is defined as "the concealment of the origins of illegally obtained money." The basic idea is relatively simple: You transmit your money to a legitimate source, such as a bank—this is called *placement*; next, the money is blended into your existing equity, such as real estate or stocks—this is called *layering*; and last, you collect your money in the form of dividends and income, which is recognized, taxed, and completely legal in the eyes of the IRS—this final step is called *integration*.

Sounds simple enough, but don't forget that plenty of people brighter than you have attempted this and failed. Again, we want to get this right and that means a fluent understanding of the mechanics of laundering money. Let's take some time to go over each of these stages in detail.

PLACEMENT

The placement phase has two primary purposes: It relieves you of holding and guarding large amounts of bulky cash and it places the money into a legitimate financial system. This is the most dangerous phase of money laundering as it calls for the use of outside parties (we call these parties *smurfs*). Smurfs are people that help take a large sum of money and distribute it, in small amounts (generally in $10,000 increments), to various accounts across numerous banks.

As an example: Let's say you are trying to launder $1,000,000 in cash. To do this you're going to need 160 individuals who are responsible for creating accounts across twenty different banks. This will allow you to avoid getting too close to the $10,000 tripwire that the IRS requires banks to impose to detect activity just like this. The commission you will pay each smurf is up to you, as is whether you decide to make your identity known.

LAYERING

The layering stage separates your ill-gotten capital from its source, thereby obscuring the audit trail and ensuring the sum of your investments (*placements*, ahem) are no longer equal to those originally received. Some of the many exploits that can be leveraged during the layering phase are currency exchanges, wire transmittal services, and domestic shell corporations set up specifically to hold or move illicit funds. These types of offshore corporations make it more difficult for the Feds to pin down where your assets originated, and can be found through a simple Google search.

Please read "Confidants and Profitable Partnerships" on page 21 for methods of finding and working with partners like smurfs and runners.

INTEGRATION

Your money is now laundered, so your goal is to find ways for that clean money to make its way back into your pocket, legally. This is done through a process called integration. The money will come back to you through seemingly legitimate legal transactions, such as dividends from savvy stock purchases, the sale of rare art or valuables, or the steady stream of income generated by your newly acquired car wash (or whatever venture you decide to embark on). The more sources you use, the faster this money will hit your accounts and the harder it will be for the authorities to follow the trail back to you.

Once you have successfully cleansed your cash you have a very big decision to make: Do you stay or do you go?

Outthinking Big Brother
and Disappearing Completely

INVENTING YOUR NEW IDENTITY

If you had the chance to start over and become whoever you wanted, who would you be? Your newfound riches will offer you the rare opportunity to shed your skin and take on a new life as someone totally different. You can have a new name, Social Security number, home address, phone number, and email address. Your social presence however, you will keep (we'll cover this soon). While we have gone over the art of disguise in previous chapters, we will focus on a more permanent solution here: a disguise that you will never have to slip out of again.

Vanishing from the public eye is no easy task, and in fact, it may not even be necessary if you've followed the steps in this book carefully. However, you may have trouble transitioning from one lifestyle to the next without the cleansing effect of shedding the old you. If you are one of these people, read on. However, if you are in any way unsure of whether you have the fortitude to erase your past and chart into the unknown, I suggest you wait until you are certain that this is what you want. Once you start this process, there is no going back.

Inventing a new identity is certainly the easy part. Perhaps you're one of those people who have already daydreamed about this sort of thing. You will need a new name and a modified look, but furthermore, you will need to take on the characteristics, mannerisms, and behaviors of your new personality. And these changes need to be permanent. This process is much more complex than a simple disguise; wigs and makeup simply will not do. You need the complete picture and to be able to prove how you got there. And to do this you need to prepare to change something you've had since the day you were born.

ACQUIRING A CLEAN SOCIAL SECURITY NUMBER

Let's start with the granddaddy of personal identifiers: your Social Security number. The Social Security number (or SSN) has become the de facto national identification number for taxation and identification purposes. To set up your bank accounts, insurance, credit cards, and even your utilities, you will need to have a valid government-assigned SSN. And since your goal is a clean slate, meaning you are literally starting over from scratch, stealing someone else's information isn't an option as all existing SSNs come with a past.

To do this we're going to exploit a few caveats in the rulebook. For instance, when a baby is born at home (as a home birth), the parents have the option to file for the new SSN in *per-*

son, rather than registering through a hospital. In addition, because not all parents stick around after a child is born, it's also possible to register as a single parent, meaning you only need *one* SSN that isn't linked to you to generate a completely new SSN. This is how you will get around involving a hospital, which would normally handle the registration of your child's SSN directly.

To get your new (rather, your *baby's* new) SSN, you're going to need *two* key documents:

1. A completed SS-5 form with the parent's Social Security number. (You can download and complete Form SS-5 directly from the SSA website.)
2. An identification card and passport for the issuing parent (you).

The tricky part here is that you're going to have to use an *existing* SSN for the parent who is filing—and it can't be your own. (Remember, anyone who decides to come snooping around must have no way of connecting the old you to the new you.) This means you're going to have to find someone whom you trust and who is willing to lend you his or her SSN—at the right price, of course. To do this properly—cleanly—you need your identity completely shielded from the person you are making this arrangement with. It protects both of you. Your name and even your look need to be changed or you run the risk of someone linking the crime to the real you, linking the real you to your business associate, and linking your business associate to the new you. For this to work you must break the connection between your old SSN and your new SSN completely.

> As a reminder for the person who is lending you her SSN, assure her that this will in no way affect her credit in the future. Bad credit associated with a child's SSN does not roll back up to the parent (or hospital for that matter) who requested it.

Last, and this is really the easiest part of all, we'll need to come up with some expertly forged documents to prove your baby's existence, along with your identification as the parent. There are many ways to fabricate documents from state identification to passports to birth certificates, and to do this you will need all of the above. For more information on how to find an expert forger please read "Fake Identification" on page 5. Once you've submitted your application, you should receive a Social Security card in six to twelve weeks. Voilà.

OTHER FORMS OF IDENTIFICATION

After getting your new SSN, you will receive a paper card in the mail that will be useful in the future for proving you are who you say you are. One of those uses will be applying for a state ID or driver's license. This is the bread and butter of an identity: the person themselves, in the flesh; a Social Security card; and a valid state identification.

Anything else you might need, from this point forward, should be attainable with these two pieces of information, from the bank accounts you set up to begin receiving transfers to the investments you make to further layer and clean your money.

But we're not quite there *yet*. There's still a little problem we need to address: The *old* you is still here.

DISINFORMATION (AND YOUR LAST GOOD-BYE)

It's time to prepare for the cathartic process of shedding (and shredding) everything—tangible or otherwise—that can reveal your true identity. This means destroying hard drives, shredding paper bills, canceling credit cards, and deleting accounts you own; such as your bank account, cell phone, insurance, cable, Internet, water, power—everything. If you own a house, car, business, whatever; it's time to find buyers. You need to space out these transactions to avoid suspicion. Whether it takes weeks or months, by the end of this process you should have nothing in your name except for one very important thing: your social networking accounts.

There is a powerful tool you will leverage to tell the story of your sudden disappearance. It's called *disinformation*, which is false information that is given to people to make them believe something or to hide the truth—both of which you will need to do to lead someone who might be trying to find you down a dead end.

You're going to start by planning a trip to some place far and remote. A place that some might even consider dangerous. Post updates in the weeks leading up to your trip expressing your excitement to explore the Amazon rain forest, or hike the trails of Machu Picchu, or sail the Panama Canal. Whatever your story is you want to make sure plenty of people are exposed to it. When you don't come back there should be a plausible reason as to why.

It's entirely up to you who you want to let in on this little secret of yours, if anyone at all. Maybe you are going with a partner in crime or maybe alone. However, if you do tell anyone or bring anyone along you must be able to trust him or her completely.

In order to produce an effective dead end, the next step in all of this is that you must actually travel to the destination you've chosen for your story. Pack what things you have left (it shouldn't be much at this point) and take a bus to the airport. You want your travels out of the city to be highly visible to help corroborate your story. Once you arrive at the far-off end to your journey, it's time to cut the cord and say good-bye to your former life forever. Every day tourists disappear—whether it's in the crowded marketplaces of Thailand or the vast Australian Outback or the frozen tundra of Russia—and so can *you*, just another vanished tourist. From this point forward you will have an entirely new identity. By doing this you are leaving any potential pathfinders leadless and with endless possibilities. This range is what I call the *scope of possibilities*, and the broader the scope the more resources it will take to shrink it. Ultimately, with so many potentials and so few leads, authorities will give up and walk away, leaving your identity to vanish into cold case ether.

Now it's time to book another flight using your *new* identity and to your *final* destination, your safe haven—your home. In many ways this is your own private funeral but also your rebirth—so celebrate! Not everyone gets a chance to start over. With the means to live any way you like, this is the part where you choose what kind of life you *want*. Will you settle down in a charming Italian villa on the Riviera and drink espressos on your balcony or live large in a London flat overlooking Hyde Park? You could vanish to a secluded island off the Caribbean coast and let the sound of waves be your alarm clock, or maybe you want to purchase a private jet to tour the globe, visiting one paradise after the next, stopping only where it's warm? Will you entertain lovers and read every classic novel? Will you learn to paint the Seine in oils? Listen to snow fall in the Alps? Will you charter your own sailboat and nap in the afternoons with the sea rocking you? Whatever it is that you want in this new life of yours, you can have, and without threat. Enjoy it. Toast to it. You've studied and worked tirelessly. Indulge your whims, you've earned it.

ACKNOWLEDGMENTS

THE CLOSE ONES

My wife and partner in everything.

My family for their creativity and support.

THE THIEVES

Mina Shokry for his on-the-ground reconnaissance in Cairo, Egypt.

Jakob Vinther for his on-the-ground report in Berlin, Germany.

Dylan Squires for teaching me about electromagnetic pulse devices.

Andrew Matthews for teaching me about radio scrambling.

Adrian Chapmanlaw for teaching me about helicopters.

Mercedes Pollmeier for teaching me about scaling buildings.

Andrew Adams for teaching me about surveillance systems.

Stefan Attaway for teaching me about mechanical chases and building construction.

Lucas Borntreger for teaching me about building construction and electrical wiring.

THE OTHERS

Mark Gottlieb for sharing my vision and for always picking up the phone.

Amanda Shih for making me sound better than I do.

Meg Leder for her inspiration and for bringing this book to life.

John Duff and the entire team at Perigee Books.

Elaine Partnow for her wonderful editing work.

Denice Au and Ross Felten for their beautiful illustrations.

Sean Petersen, Jason Leon, and Brian McWilliams, for their support and good will.

Michael Bayouth for showing me how to trace.

Ryan Ford for his theifdom iconography (theryanford.com).

All of the people who wished to stay anonymous (there were many).

ABOUT THE AUTHOR

Taylor Bayouth was born in Los Angeles, California, where he currently lives with his wife and daughter. On any given day you will find him creating something new—whether it's art, technology, literature, or his next museum heist.